Simple Predictive A

Using Excel to Solve Business Problems

Curtis Seare

© 2010, 2019 by Vault Analytics LLC
All rights reserved. First edition 2010.
Second edition 2019

Printed in the United States of America
27 26 25 24 23 22 21 20 19   2 3 4 5

Table of Contents

Section I: Background Information

Why Use Predictive Analytics?

How to Use This Guide

Analysis Fundamentals

Method for Creating Predictive Models

Section II: Predictive Models

How to Choose an Appropriate Model

Regression

- Correlation
- Linear Regression
- Multivariate
- Exponential Regression
- Logarithmic Regression
- Polynomial Regression
- Time Series

Logistic Regression

ANOVA

- t-Test
- One-Way ANOVA
- Two-Way ANOVA

Chi-Square

Why Use Predictive Analytics?

Strategy Development

Predictive analytics is an indispensable tool for strategy development. In any good strategy, there are three elements: a set of assumptions, a set of actions that need to be taken, and a set of desired outcomes. The outcomes are achieved as a result of the actions being executed and the assumptions being true. In essence, we say: Assuming A is true, if we do B we will achieve C.

Predictive analytics helps out with all three of the steps considered above. Statistical tests tell us if our assumptions are correct and predictive models fit to historic data help us quantify what the result will be with a given set of inputs. The value of having a statistically valid predictive model in strategy development is that you can know what you need to do to produce the best results.

Further, simple predictive models are not above most people's abilities to produce. It requires some understanding of statistics, as well as various predictive modeling techniques. This guide provides you with both the statistical basics you need to know, as well as a process that can be followed to choose and implement an appropriate predictive modeling technique for your given situation. It stays admittedly away from many technicalities so that focus can be placed on just the information that is necessary to get a predictive model built and in working order.

Example Business Questions Answered

The reason we do predictive analytics is to solve business problems. Accordingly, here are some example business questions that can be answered with each of the predictive models described in this guide.

Regression

Correlation

- From a large database of customer data, which factors are associated with response rates?
- From all the metrics on our website, which ones are associated with purchases on the site?
- From all the medical data collected in a patient sample, which factors are associated with high blood pressure?

Linear Regression

- If we send out 'x' number of mail pieces to a target customer segment, how many sales will we get in return?
- If we sell 'x' number of product A, how much can we expect to sell of product B?
- If 'x' number of people sign up for this promotional program, how many extra sales can we expect?

Multivariate Linear Regression

- How many subscriptions can we expect to get by spending specific amounts of time in various social media marketing channels?
- What is the optimal word count, number of graphics, and number of topics covered in our weekly newsletter in order to get the most click-throughs?

Exponential Regression

- How long does it typically take for one of our marketing campaigns to go viral?

Logarithmic Regression

- At what point in time will we see a significant decrease in responses from our mailer campaign?
- How long should we provide training on a specific task until we start seeing significantly less marginal benefit?

Polynomial Regression

- What is the appropriate amount of customer contacts per month to maximize sales?
- What should we set the price at in order to sell the maximum amount of a given product?

Time Series and Forecasting

- How many sales are we likely to have in the next year?
- How much do the specific months of the year affect our close rates?

Logistic Regression

- Will someone of a given age respond to our marketing campaign?
- Will someone purchase this product given a certain price?
- Will someone who has not logged into your product for a certain amount of days cancel?
- Will someone who has spent a given amount of time on your website purchase something?

ANOVA

t-Test

- Does gender affect the sales rate of our products?
- Does this medical treatment affect the blood pressure of our patients?
- Does this training course increase the efficiency of our staff?

One-Way ANOVA

- Which customer segments for a specific marketing campaign have the highest response rates?
- Which version of a mailer piece has the best response rate?
- Which traffic source to our website has the highest propensity for lead generation?

Two-Way ANOVA

- What is the best combination of marketing channel and product offering to get the highest sales rates?

Chi-Square

- Out of all of our customer segments, which ones are the most likely to buy specific products?
- What groups of people are most likely to be re-admitted to the hospital within 60 days?

How to Use This Guide

This guide is designed to be as simple as possible, giving you the critical information you need to create, use, and validate various simple predictive models.

First, some analysis fundamentals are provided. These are the basics of doing good and accurate analysis, and it will be important to keep these principles in mind as you create predictive models.

Second, a process is provided that will allow you to follow some easy, predefined steps to creating your own predictive models. This is a 'big-picture' process flow meant to give you a basic procedure to follow no matter what type of predictive model you need to create.

Last, the guide gives you an in-depth look into various predictive modeling techniques, organized according to the type of data you have and the type of question you're trying to answer. This section makes up the bulk of the book, and each of the models is explained by telling you what the predictive model looks like, what it can be used for, the assumptions necessary to use the model, a process to follow to create it (including step-by-step instructions in Excel), an explanation of some common errors to watch for, a section on analyzing your results, and a section listing a nonparametric counterpart test to use if the conditions for normality are not met in the data.

Preparing to Use Excel

Excel is used in the specific "How To" sections, as it is the most ubiquitous piece of software with statistical capabilities. Excel is admittedly limited in these statistical capabilities, but it affords the basic functionality necessary to create and validate simple predictive models.

Two add-ins are used throughout this guide to aid you in doing the necessary statistical tests for each predictive model. They are the Data Analysis ToolPak and the Solver Add-in. These add-ins come with Excel, but you must activate them before you can use them. Some older versions of Excel do not include the Data Analysis ToolPak; however, you can use a third-party add-in noted on this Office support page.

To activate both of them, simply go to the Tools menu and click "Excel Add-ins". In older versions, you may need to go to the home menu and click *Excel Options*.

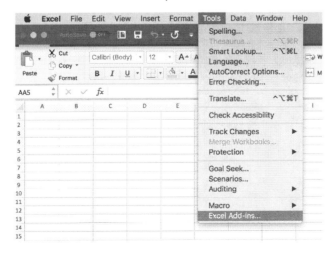

Next, check both 'Analysis ToolPak' and 'Solver Add-In' (or Solver.Xlam), and click 'OK'

Analysis Fundamentals

Although an entire book could be written about the fundamentals of good analysis, here we will cover just two fundamentals that are the most critical. These two basics are **seeing the data in context** and **segmentation**.

Seeing the Data in Context

Understanding what the data are telling you within the context of the business situation being analyzed is extremely important. This will help you avoid making faulty conclusions and keep your analysis appropriate for the business question being answered. The best way to learn this fundamental is to see it in action, so we will take an example.

We will look at a type of direct mail campaign analysis. We want to know how many calls are expected to come into our call center after we execute the campaign. First, we take some historical data showing us the percentage of total calls coming in according to the number of days after starting a mail campaign, shown below.

Days After Mailing	% Total Incoming Calls
1	1%
2	3%
3	4%
4	12%
5	19%
6	26%
7	31%
8	36%
9	41%

After creating a scatter plot of the data, we try to fit a logarithmic regression line as a model, shown below.

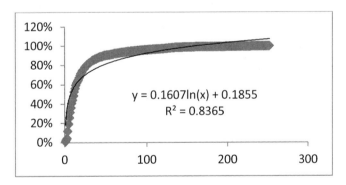

$y = 0.1607\ln(x) + 0.1855$
$R^2 = 0.8365$

Even though the R^2 tells us that the fit is good, the model may not be the best way to explain this data when the context and purpose of this analysis are considered. We want the model to be able to predict what percentage of total calls will come in from a mailing campaign so we can staff the call center. If I were to use the equation above as the model, I would be predicting low values for incoming calls between about day 20 and 100, and high values thereafter. Because of this error, we would not be staffing the call center correctly.

To create a better model, I would consider the fact that, in this context, it is not necessary to fit a trend model to the entire data set. Consider the following model, which can be used to predict the percentage of total calls coming in between days four and 35 after the mailing campaign:

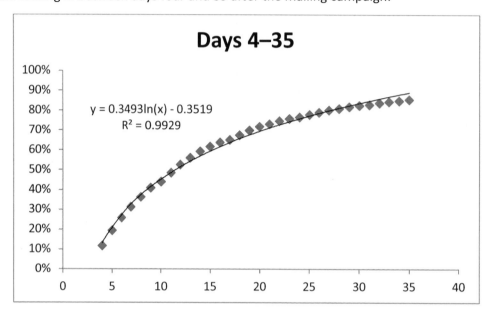

You will notice that this trend model does not contain the same high and low errors as the previous model did. Further, upon doing some calculations on the data in the spreadsheet, we know that anything before day four makes up for just 8% of all calls, and anything after day 35 makes up for just 15% of all calls. I have highlighted with a model the time period of the biggest growth to the call percentage, while summarizing the remaining percentages on either side. This will give just the right amount of information needed to staff the call center, while minimizing the errors made trying to fit a single trend model to the entire data set.

The point here is to look at the data in the context of the purpose of the analysis. What are you going to use the predictive model for? Is it necessary to fit a model to the entire data set? How exact do you need to be with the prediction? What is the most important part of the data set to model? These questions are important to consider when performing analysis.

Segmentation

The second fundamental of analysis is the practice of segmenting the data. As with seeing the data in context, this is best described with an example. Consider the analysis presented below, which shows a linear regression model to predict how much someone will likely donate to your cause according to their age.

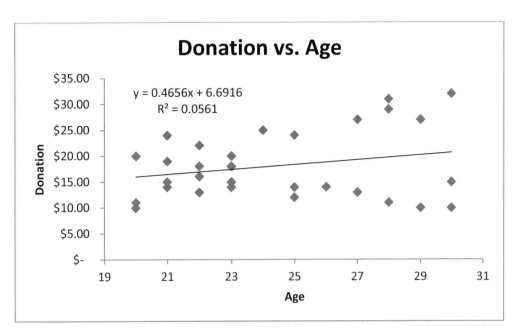

The fit of the model is extremely weak, and there seems to be no relationship between donation and age. However, this data was taken and aggregated from two different cities, Boston and New York. If we separate out the data according to those two cities (otherwise known as *segmenting* by them), we get the following when we run a regression analysis:

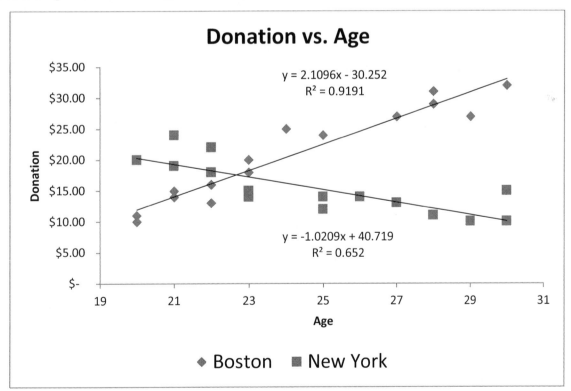

By segmenting the data first, we notice that there is, in fact, a relationship between donation and age, but that relationship differs depending on what city you are in.

Data Cleaning

This topic could be a book in itself, but we'll at least mention it here. Data preparation entails working with the data to get it into a format that can be used for analysis. Two major considerations of data preparation are data cleaning and feature engineering.

Data Cleaning

This refers to the activity of making sure your data is accurate and complete and that missing data is handled appropriately. Some common things to check for are duplication of values, values that don't make sense (for example, negative values in a column that represents age), or an incomplete data set (for example, if you are analyzing a year's worth of data, you would want to make sure you aren't missing any months or weeks).

You will also want to handle missing values. For example, if you have a column that shows product prices and there are some blanks, how will you interpret that? Does a blank mean the price was zero, or is the value just missing from the data set because it was not entered? Maybe you want to throw out those particular rows that have the blank values or throw out the entire column or guess the value is zero or make a guess based on the average price of similar products. What you do will depend on the context of the data.

Feature Engineering

This refers to creating new columns in your data set that might be valuable to use in your analysis. As a basic example, you may want to subtract cost from revenue to get a profit column or calculate a percent of total. This activity can get very complicated as your analysis gets more sophisticated, but even basic additions like the ones already mentioned can make a significant improvement in your analysis.

Method for Creating Predictive Models

Outline

1. Choose a predictive model according to the business question.
2. Check to see if all the conditions for the model are met.
3. Carry out the analysis.
4. Check for statistical significance and fit.
5. Validate the predictive model.
6. Refine the predictive model.

1. Choose a Predictive Model

Once you have a business question in mind, you must look at what kinds of variables you will be working with in order to answer this question. The models in this guide will help you with the following four situations, which are fairly comprehensive:

- *Predict a quantitative outcome with quantitative explanatory variables*
- *Predict a "yes" or "no" outcome with quantitative explanatory variables*
- *Predict a quantitative outcome according to categorical explanatory variables*
- *Predict a categorical outcome according to categorical explanatory variables*

The difference between quantitative and categorical variables is described below.

Quantitative Variable

Anything that can be measured or counted is a quantitative variable. This includes things such as heights, distances, weights, number of items, etc. Because these variables are numerical, you can perform mathematical operations on them, such as addition, multiplication, division, and the like. Below is an example of what quantitative variables look like in a spreadsheet:

Sales	Costs	Distance (mi)
457	$ 24.00	5.4
514	$ 57.00	2.4
234	$ 84.00	2.1
541	$ 54.00	4.6
465	$ 74.00	6.2
451	$ 71.00	3.8

Above, the variables are *Sales*, *Costs*, and *Distance*, each followed by the data points that make them up.

Categorical (or Qualitative) Variable

These variables use categories to classify individuals. This can include things such as gender (male, female), industry (chemical, finance, construction, etc.), zip code, and others. Below is an example of what categorical variables look like in a spreadsheet:

Channel	Product	Color
Internet	Product A	Blue
Direct Mail	Product B	Red
Tele Sales	Product C	Green

Above, the categorical variables are *Channel*, *Product*, and *Color*, and each are followed by the values that make them up.

2. Check Conditions

Each statistical test has a set of conditions that must be met in order for it to be valid. These are listed in each of the sections describing the different statistical predictive models. Make sure all of the conditions hold true before and during the analysis, or your conclusions may be faulty.

3. Carry Out the Analysis

Each section describing a predictive model has a process to follow with step-by-step instructions in Excel. Be sure to look at the warnings (also included in each section) as you are performing the analysis to make sure everything turns out right.

4. Check for Significance and Fit

The two statistical values described below are useful for almost all of the predictive models described in this guide. They will help you know the validity and fit of your model. Any other statistics that will help validate the predictive model are included in the individual sections.

p-value

The p-value is used to know if your model is statistically significant (meaning it can reasonably be used to infer something about the entire population, beyond your data sample). It represents the probability that you will be incorrect by saying your predictive model is valid. The lower that value is, therefore, the greater probability you have that the predictive model is useful for the population. Values are between 0 and 1, and in general a model that has a p-value less than .05 (So a 5% chance your model cannot be used to infer something about the population) is considered statistically significant. This is the level of significance used throughout this guide.

R^2

The R^2 value is used to show how well your predictive model fits the data. In other words, it tells you how well the model can predict the outcomes of your sample. Values are between 0 and 1. In a business setting, a rule of thumb is that values between .8 and 1 show a strong fit, .6-.8 a good fit, .4-.6 show a questionable fit, and under .4 shows there that the model is not a good fit for the data. If the fit of your model is not high enough, you can try three things:

- Try a different predictive model to fit the data
- Add more or different explanatory variables to your predictive model

- Break the data you are testing into smaller categories (a practice known as segmentation), and then build separate models for each of the categories

If you are using a model containing more than one explanatory variable, you will want to use the R^2 *adjusted* to give you the correct value for this statistic.

5. Validate the Predictive Model

After you have a statistically significant, well-fit model, it's important to do one last test to check its performance. You do this by applying the predictive model to data that you've collected, but that was not used in the creation of the model. There are several sophisticated ways of model validation, but one simple method for doing this is to, before creating the predictive model, randomly split the data into two sections. You could for example build your predictive model on 80% of the data, and then see how the model fits the other 20%. Be careful to ensure that there is no bias in your method of dividing the data, it must be a completely random split to work.

6. Refine the Predictive Model

Now you are ready to apply the predictive model to new data. As you continue to use it, it is important to check its performance (as data and circumstances change, your model may become less accurate over time—this is known as model drift). This way your model will stay current with the changing environment.

How to Choose an Appropriate Model

Predict a quantitative outcome with quantitative explanatory variables:

Regression

- Correlation
- Linear Regression
- Multivariate
- Exponential Regression
- Logarithmic Regression
- Polynomial Regression
- Time Series

Predict a *yes* or *no* outcome with quantitative explanatory variables:

Logistic Regression

Predict a quantitative outcome according to categorical explanatory variables:

ANOVA

- t-Test
- One-Way ANOVA
- Two-Way ANOVA

Predict a categorical outcome according to categorical explanatory variables:

Chi-Square

Regression Overview

Predictive Model

Regression models always take the form of an equation, with *x* representing the input, or explanatory variable, and *y* representing the output, or response variable. It is one of the most common types of predictive models. It allows the practitioner to predict the outcome of a quantitative variable according to one or more quantitative inputs.

Choosing the Appropriate Model

The type of regression you choose to use will be according to the type of relationship the variables exhibit. (You can see this relationship visually by making a scatter plot.)

- **Correlation**, **Linear Regression**, and **Multivariate Linear Regression** all describe a linear relationship between variables:

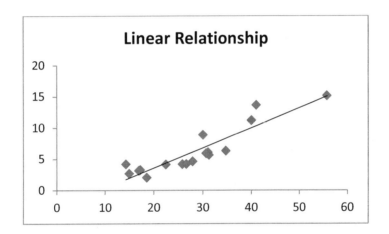

- **Exponential Regression** describes an exponential relationship:

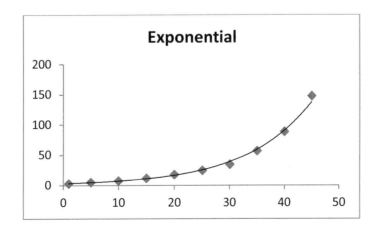

- **Logarithmic Regression** describes a logarithmic relationship:

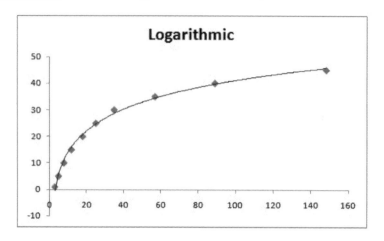

- **Polynomial Regression** describes a polynomial relationship:

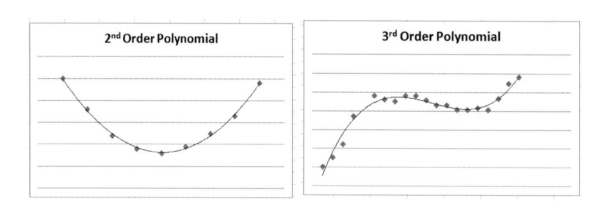

- **Time Series** describes a trend and/or seasonal relationship:

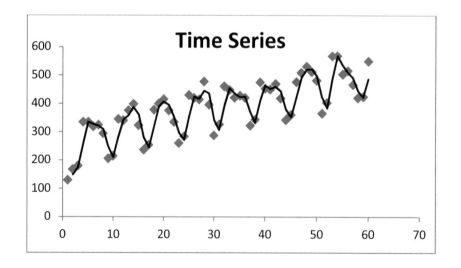

General Regression Conditions

The following conditions must hold for all the statistical tests described in this section:

- The x and y must be quantitative.
- Y-values must have a normal distribution.
    - To figure this out, you will look at a residual plot, which shows how far each data point deviates from your model. We use a slightly modified form of this plot to normalize the data, called a standardized residual plot.
    - On a <u>standardized residual plot</u>, you can identify that y has a normal distribution if you see more values close to zero and less further away, (This is true in the plot below.)
    - If your sample size is over 50, it's less important that this condition is met.

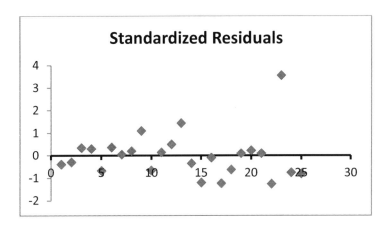

- The y values must have the same variance around each x.
    - Looking at the <u>best fit line</u> on a scatter plot—this condition is not met if y output values within specific ranges of x tend to be further or closer from the best fit line than all other y value. (Below you can see that the y values spread out further from the best fit line as x gets larger, so the criteria is not met.)

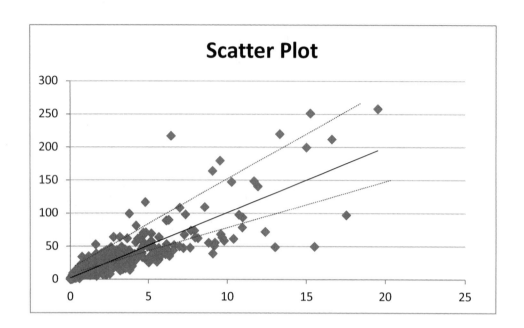

- The data must be homogeneous. You can look at the scatter plot to make sure of this. (You can't have large spans of x values with no data, so the data below is *not* homogeneous.)

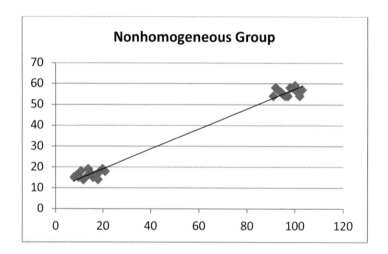

- The residuals must be independent. You can tell this from the Standardized Residual plot—if there is no pattern in the data (for instance, an upward trend), then they are independent. (The only pattern that is all right to see in the data is that more values are closer to zero than further away. This does not negate independence). The plot below shows independence, as there is no pattern. If this condition is not met, you may need to run a time series analysis. (The only test in this section that does not require this condition to be met.)

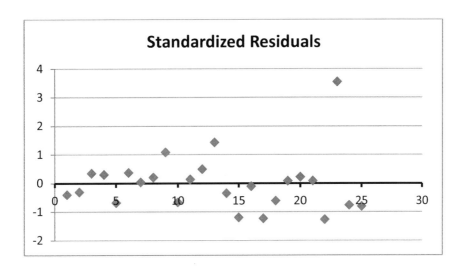

How to Check Conditions in Excel

- To make a **scatter plot**—highlight the two data sets of interest, then click *insert > scatter > choose upper left option*

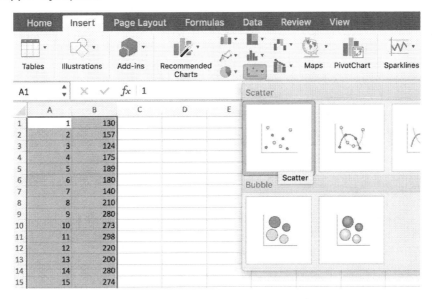

- To get a **best fit line**—right click a data point on the scatter plot, click *Add Trendline*, and then choose the line that best represents the data.

- To get a **standardized residual plot**, click *Data > Data Analysis > Regression*.

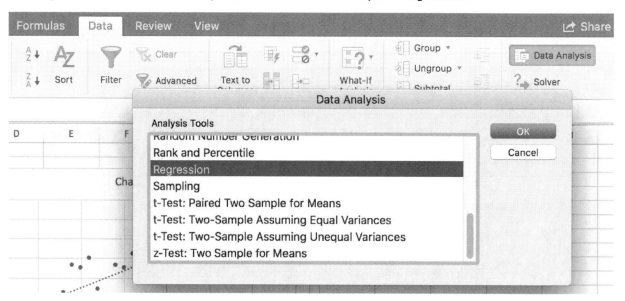

- Then highlight the x and y input ranges, and check boxes for *standardized residuals*. Then click *OK*.

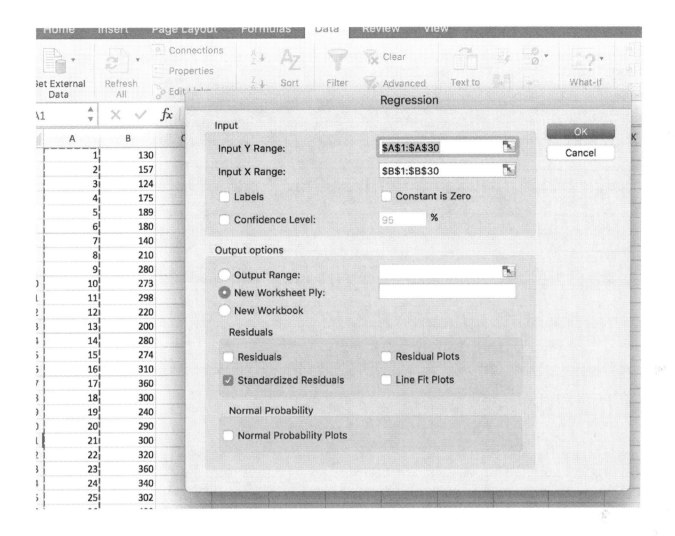

With the output of this step, highlight *Observation* and *Standard Residuals* and make a scatter plot, as seen below.

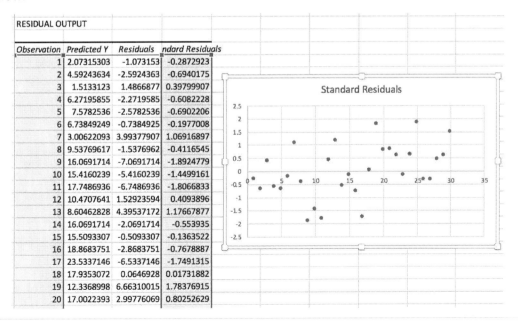

Regression General Warnings

- Watch for outliers. You can find them on the standardized residual plot—generally points higher than 3 or lower than -3 are considered outliers. (These numbers represent standard deviations from the mean.) You can see an example of one below:

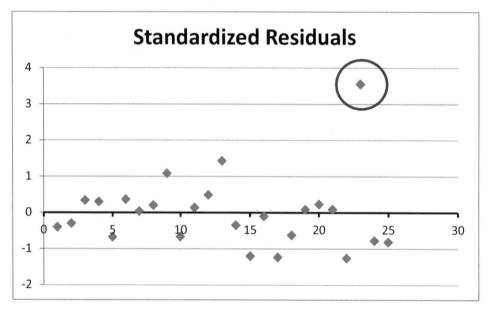

If you have outliers in the data, do the following:
- Check and make sure there wasn't a mistake in the collection of the data. If there was, then throw out the outlier from the data set.
- If there was no mistake, it may not be ethical or accurate to throw it out because it is a real point of data. It's best to run the regression with and without the outliers, present both results, and give an interpretation of what the outliers may signify.

Correlation

Uses

Correlation is used to find which quantitative variables are associated with each other. It is a preparatory analysis before creating predictive linear regression models. Correlation analysis is especially useful in crunching a lot of data quickly in order to find where relationships exist. Once these relationships are found, it is easier to know what variables to use for a linear predictive model.

Example Questions Answered

- From a large database of customer behavior measures, which factors are associated with response rates?
- From all the metrics on our website, which ones are associated with purchases on the site?
- From all the medical data collected in a patient sample, which factors are associated with blood pressure?

Conditions

- The x and y variables must be quantitative.
- The x and y variables must have a linear relationship. (On a scatter plot, it looks like you could draw a line through them, as seen below.)

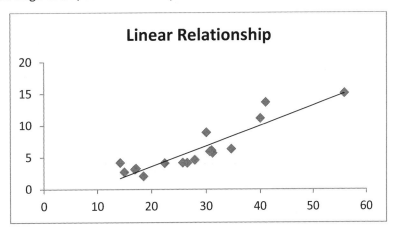

- Check for normality. (If normality is not met, you should use a nonparametric test unless your sample is over 50.)
    - The y values must have a normal distribution.
        - On a standardized residual plot, this is true if you see more values close to zero and less further away. (See 'General Regression Conditions' for graphic.)
        - If your sample size is over 50, it's less important that this condition is met.
    - The y values must have the same variance around each x.
        - Look at the best fit line on the scatter plot; this condition is not met if higher or lower values of x tend to be further from the best fit line than other values. (See 'General Regression Conditions' for graphic.)
- The data must be a homogeneous group. (See 'General Regression Conditions' for graphics.)

- The residuals must be independent. You can tell this from the Standardized Residual plot—if there is no pattern in the data (for instance, an upward trend), then they are independent. (See 'General Regression Conditions' for graphic.) If this condition is not met, you may need to run a time series analysis.

"How to" in Excel

1. First, run the correlation: click *Data > Data Analysis > Correlation*. Check the box for "Labels in First Row," and highlight all the data you want to test for correlation (including column labels). Then hit "OK." You will get back a matrix of r values. The values will be between -1 and 1. The closer the 1 or -1, the higher the positive or negative correlation, respectively. Values closer to zero are not very correlated. Below, the values that have a high correlation are highlighted, showing which data sets are associated with each other.

	Column 1	Column 2	Column 3	Column 4
Column 1	1			
Column 2	-0.05631	1		
Column 3	0.892018	-0.09966	1	
Column 4	-0.28892	0.756836	-0.24352	1

2. Next, make scatter plots of the correlated data sets: highlight the two data sets of interest, then hit *insert > scatter >* then choose upper left option
3. To fit a line on the scatter plot, right click a data point on the plot and click *add trendline >* choose *linear >* then choose *close*. This will give you a better idea on how well the data are correlated.

Analysis

Correlation Coefficient, r (Pearson's coefficient)

This measure shows the strength and direction of the correlation between two quantitative variables.

- Positive values mean that as x increases, so does y.
- Negative values mean that as x increases, y decreases.
- Values are always between -1 and 1.
- Rule of thumb for ranges in a business context are as follows:
    - .8–1 means a very strong correlation
    - .6–.8 means strong correlation
    - .4–.6 means some correlation
    - Less than .4 means little or no correlation

Scatterplot

This shows graphically the strength, direction, and consistency of the association.

Warnings

- You cannot predict anything or say one variable is dependent upon another in this analysis; you can merely state how strongly two variables are or are not correlated to each other.
- Watch for Outliers.

Nonparametric Counterpart

If the normality condition is not met and your sample size is small, you may need to use the nonparametric counterpart to this test, which is known as Spearman's rank. For the Spearman's Rank test there is no need for a normal distribution, the data don't need to have a linear relationship, and it can be used with ordinal data (explained below),

Ordinal Data

These are qualitative variables with a special feature: they can be ordered and given a numerical value. For example, if a survey asks you to rate your customer experience on a scale from 1 as "very poor" to 5 as "excellent," it is collecting *ordinal* data. The numbers 1–5 are categories related to how good the experience was, and their order holds meaning. In simple categorical variables, this is not true. (You cannot order *male* and *female* in any way to give added meaning.)

Linear Regression

Predictive Model

The predictive model you will create in a linear regression analysis is an equation, shown below:

$$y = Ax + B$$

Above, *y* is the outcome variable, and *x* is the explanatory variable. *A* is known as the coefficient of *x*, and B is a constant. The regression test will allow you to find the appropriate coefficient and constant values to define the relationship between y and x, allowing you to predict outcomes according to specific *x* values.

Uses

Linear regression predicts the value of one response variable, y, given the value of one explanatory variable, x. It is often done directly after a correlation analysis.

Example Questions Answered

- If we send out x number of mail pieces to a target customer segment, how many sales will we get in return?
- If we sell x number of product A, how much can we expect to sell of product B?
- If x number of people sign up for this promotional program, how many extra donations can we expect?

Conditions

- The x and y variables must be quantitative.
- The x and y variables must have a linear relationship.
- Check for normality. (If normality is not met and your sample size is less than 50, you should use a nonparametric test like the one suggested at the end of this section.)
    - The y values must have a normal distribution.
        - On a standardized residual plot, this is true if you see more values close to zero and less further away. (See 'General Regression Conditions' for graphic.)
        - If your sample size is over 50, it's less important that this condition is met.
    - The y values must have the same variance around each x.
        - Look at the best fit line on the scatter plot; this condition is not met if higher or lower values of x tend to be further from the best fit line than other values. (See 'General Regression Conditions' for graphic.)
- They must have a homogeneous group (see 'General Regression Conditions' for graphics)
- The residuals must be independent. You can tell this from the Standardized Residual plot—if there is no pattern in the data (for instance, an upward trend), then they are independent. (See 'General Regression Conditions' for graphic.) If this condition is not met, you may need to run a time series analysis.

"How to" in Excel

1. To make a scatter plot, highlight the two data sets of interest, then select *insert > scatter*. Choose the upper left option. If you notice a linear relationship, continue with this method.
2. Do the regression: *Data > Data Analysis > Regression*, then highlight the explanatory variable for *Input X Range*, and the response variable for *Input Y Range*. Check the box for *Standardized Residuals > OK*.
3. The p-values, R^2, and coefficients of interest are highlighted below in the regression output.

SUMMARY OUTPUT

Regression Statistics	
Multiple R	0.910202944
R Square	0.828469399
Adjusted R Squ	0.821011547
Standard Error	153.8446467
Observations	25

ANOVA

	df	SS	MS	F	Significance F
Regression	1	2629223.328	2629223	111.0869	2.80942E-10
Residual	23	544368.0324	23668.18		
Total	24	3173591.36			

	Coefficients	Standard Error	t Stat	P-value	Lower 95%	Upper 95%	Lower 95.0%	Upper 95.0%
Intercept	189.5072973	63.84843674	2.96808	0.006887	57.42674345	321.58785	57.4267434	321.5878511
X Variable 1	0.050958119	0.004834839	10.53978	2.81E-10	0.040956492	0.0609597	0.04095649	0.060959746

(The predictive model for the above output would be y = .051x + 189.518)

Analysis

p-value

There will be a p-value for the coefficient and the intercept, and both must be below .05 for the predictive model to be completely validated.

R^2

This shows the percentage of variability in *y* that is explained by *x* in the predictive equation. If the value is equal to 1, that means all the variability in *y* is explained perfectly. (Don't ever expect this to happen.)

Confidence Interval

Excel gives you 'Lower 95%' and 'Upper 95%' values for both the intercept and the coefficients. Statistically, you are 95% sure that the true value of either the intercept or the coefficient lies within these ranges. These values are highlighted below:

	Coefficients	Standard Error	t Stat	P-value	Lower 95%	Upper 95%
Intercept	189.5072973	63.84843674	2.968080457	0.006887	57.42674345	321.587851
X Variable 1	0.050958119	0.004834839	10.53977524	2.81E-10	0.040956492	0.06095975

With the above data, I can say that I am 95% sure that the true value (the value that would be obtained if the data was fit on the entire population, not just a sample) of the intercept of my equation lies between 57 and 321. I can also say that I am 95% sure that the true value of the x coefficient lies between .04 and .06.

Warnings

- Don't predict responses in *y* for an *x* that is outside the range of the data you built the model on. You can't be sure the relationship will hold outside this range.
- Watch for Outliers.

Nonparametric Counterpart

If the normality condition is not met, you may want to use the nonparametric counterpart to this test. One popular nonparametric test that can replace any parametric regression test is MARSplines (Multivariate Adaptive Regression Splines). It doesn't impose the condition that any specific type of relationship exists between the variables (such as linear or exponential), can be used with multiple explanatory variables, and can even predict multiple outcome variables.

Multivariate Linear Regression

Predictive Model

The predictive model you will create in a multivariate linear regression analysis is an equation, an example of which is shown below:

$$y = Ax_1 + Bx_2 + Cx_3 + D$$

Above, y is the outcome variable, and x_1, x_2, and x_3 are the explanatory variables. A, B, and C are known as the coefficients of x_1, x_2, and x_3, respectively. D is a constant. The regression test will allow you to find the appropriate coefficient and constant values to define the relationship between y and any number of x variables, allowing you to predict outcomes with specific x values.

It is important to note that you can use any number of x variables; the predictive model is not limited to 3 as shown in the equation above.

Uses

Multivariate linear regression predicts the value of a response variable, y, given the values of two or more explanatory variables (x_1, x_2, x_3, etc.).

Example Questions Answered

- How many subscriptions can we expect to get by spending specific amounts of time in various social-media marketing channels?
- What is the optimal word count, number of graphics, and number of topics covered in our weekly newsletter in order to get the most click-throughs?

Conditions

- All variables must be quantitative.
- All variables must have a linear relationship.
- Check for normality. (If normality is not met and your sample size is less than 50, you should use a nonparametric test like the one suggested at the end of this section.)
    - The Y values must have a normal distribution.
        - On a standardized residual plot, this is true if you see more values close to zero and less further away (see 'General Regression Conditions' for graphic)
        - If your sample size is over 50, it's less important that this condition is met
    - The Y values must have the same variance around each x.
        - Look at the best fit line on the scatter plot; this condition is not met if higher or lower values of x tend to be further from the best fit line than other values. (See 'General Regression Conditions' for graphic.)
- They must have a homogeneous group. (See 'General Regression Conditions' for graphics.)
- The residuals must be independent. You can tell this from the Standardized Residual plot—if there is no pattern in the data (for instance, an upward trend), then they are independent. (See

'General Regression Conditions' for graphic.) If this condition is not met, you may need to run a time series analysis.

"How to" in Excel

1. Run a correlation on all of the x values and the y value you are thinking of using in your multivariate regression. This does two things:
    - It quickly shows you which of the x variables correlate well with the y values, so you know which ones to use in the multivariate regression.
    - It shows you which x variables are correlated to each other so you can avoid multicolinearity. (If two or more *x* variables are highly correlated with each other, they should not be included in the same multivariate regression. Use only one of these variables for a given model.)
2. To run the regression: select *Data > Data Analysis > Regression*. highlight the data sets for all explanatory variable for x_1, x_2, etc., for the *input X range* and the data set for the response variable, *y*, for the *input y range >* check the box for *Standardized Residuals > OK*
3. The p-values, R^2 adjusted, and coefficients of interest are highlighted below in the regression output. If the p-values of any of the x variables are over .05, they are not significant, and the regression should be rerun without them.

SUMMARY OUTPUT

Regression Statistics	
Multiple R	0.91803485
R Square	0.842787986
Adjusted R Square	0.828495985
Standard Error	150.5937778
Observations	25

ANOVA

	df	SS	MS	F	Significance F
Regression	2	2674664.67	1337332	58.96921	1.44992E-09
Residual	22	498926.6898	22678.49		
Total	24	3173591.36			

	Coefficients	Standard Error	t Stat	P-value	Lower 95%	Upper 95%
Intercept	-106.2313421	218.0725451	-0.48714	0.630979	-558.486118	346.0234341
X Variable 1	0.05542885	0.005689761	9.74186	1.94E-09	0.043629009	0.067228692
X Variable 2	8.028427062	5.671682581	1.415528	0.170915	-3.73392264	19.79077676

(Supposing all p-values were significant, the predictive model for the above output would read $y = .055x_1 + 8.03 x_2 - 106.23$.)

4. If you want to find the optimal input *x* values to give you a desired value for the response variable, *y*, (for instance, your x variables may be *television advertising spending* and *web*

advertising spending, and you want to know the optimal mix of spending to give you the greatest sales outcome) you can use the Solver function in Excel:

- a. First, set up some cells to use Solver:
    - i. Enter guess values for each explanatory variable, as shown below highlighted in blue. (Don't worry about being too exact with the guesses. You just need something in the right ballpark.)
    - ii. Then type in the predictive equation using the coefficient and guess cells, as shown below highlighted in orange. (Remember, the format of the predictive equation you are using is y = Ax$_1$ + Bx$_2$ +C .)

	A	B	C	D	E	F	G
1	SUMMARY OUTPUT						
2							
3	*Regression Statistics*						
4	Multiple R	0.91803485		X 1 guess	25		
5	R Square	0.842787986		X 2 guess	12		
6	Adjusted R Square	0.828495985		Y (output)	=B18*E4+B19*E5+B17		
7	Standard Error	150.5937778					
8	Observations	25					
9							
10	ANOVA						
11		df	SS	MS	F	Significance F	
12	Regression	2	2674664.67	1337332.3	58.96921	1.44992E-09	
13	Residual	22	498926.6898	22678.486			
14	Total	24	3173591.36				
15							
16		Coefficients	Standard Error	t Stat	P-value	Lower 95%	Upper 95
17	Intercept	-106.2313421	218.0725451	-0.4871376	0.630979	-558.486118	346.0234:
18	X Variable 1	0.05542885	0.005689761	9.7418598	1.94E-09	0.043629009	0.0672286
19	X Variable 2	8.028427062	5.671682581	1.4155283	0.170915	-3.73392264	19.790776
20							

- b. Click *Data > Solver*
    - i. Set the *Set Objective* input box to the cell where you input the predictive equation (in the above case, E6).
    - ii. Input what kind of output value you want to find (the Max, Min, or a specific value) to the right of 'To:'
    - iii. Enter the cell range that has the *x* value guesses in the *By Changing Cells* field (above, E4 and E5).

iv. Add any constraints necessary for each *x* variable (for instance, if x_1 represents advertising cost, a constraint could be to keep that number under a certain budgeted amount).
v. Click *Solve*
vi. Solver will change your guess in the Excel sheet automatically to give you the desired result in your Objective field.

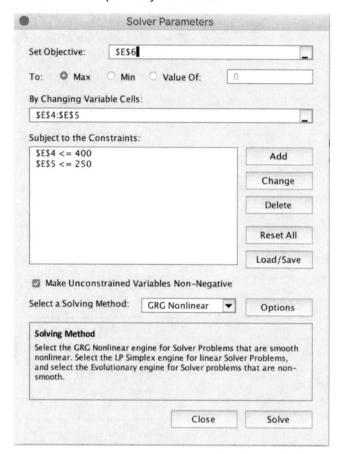

Analyze the Results

p-value

If any of the coefficients or the intercept has a p-value that is greater than .05, that specific coefficient or constant is not valid in predicting y. It should not be used in the predictive equation.

R^2 *Adjusted*

The percentage of variability in *y* that is explained by the *x* variables. Here you want to use the adjusted value, because it corrects for the fact that you have more than one explanatory variable.

Confidence Interval

See the confidence interval section under *Linear Regression* to see how to find the confidence interval.

Coefficients

The magnitude of the coefficients tells you how important each of the corresponding variables are in the predictive model. The higher the magnitude of the coefficient, the more weight its corresponding variable carries in predicting the response variable, and thus should receive more consideration.

Warnings

- Be aware of **multicolinearity**, or using two or more x variables that are correlated to each other in the same predictive equation. Make sure you do a correlation analysis of all the x variables you are using in the model to ensure they are not correlated to each other.
- Don't predict responses in y for an x that is outside the range of the data you built the model on. You can't be sure the relationship will hold outside this range.
- Watch for Outliers.

Nonparametric Counterpart

If the normality condition is not met, you may want to use the nonparametric counterpart to this test. One popular nonparametric test that can replace any parametric regression test is MARSplines (Multivariate Adaptive Regression Splines). It doesn't impose the condition that any specific type of relationship exists between the variables (such as linear or exponential), can be used with multiple explanatory variables, and can even predict multiple outcome variables.

Exponential Regression

Predictive Model

The predictive model you will create for an exponential regression analysis looks like the following:

$$y = e^{(Ax + B)}$$

Above, *y* is the outcome variable, and *x* is the explanatory variable. *A* is known as the coefficient of *x*, and *B* is a constant. The value *e* is the natural logarithm base, approximately equal to 2.718. This regression test will allow you to find the appropriate coefficient and constant values to define the relationship between y and x, allowing you to predict outcomes with specific x values.

Uses

Exponential regression is used to predict the response, y, from an explanatory variable, x, when x and y have an exponential relationship.

Example Questions Answered

- How long will does it typically take for one of our marketing campaigns to go viral?

Conditions

- The x and y variables must be quantitative.
- The relationship between x and y must be exponential, or curved, as seen in the two scatter plots below.

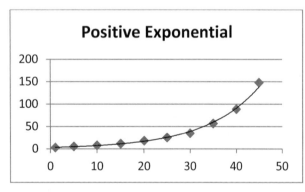
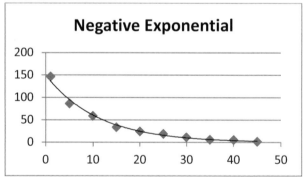

- *The exponential relationship will be transformed into a linear relationship* (see process below), *and for that linear relationship, all the conditions of Linear Regression analysis must hold* (repeated below).
- Check for normality. (If normality is not met and your sample size is less than 50, you should use a nonparametric test like the one suggested at the end of this section.)
  - The y values must have a normal distribution.
    - On a standardized residual plot, this is true if you see more values close to zero and less further away. (See 'General Regression Conditions' for graphic.)
    - If your sample size is over 50, it's less important that this condition is met.
  - The y values must have the same variance around each x.

- Look at the best fit line on the scatter plot; this condition is not met if higher or lower values of x tend to be further from the best fit line than other values. (See 'General Regression Conditions' for graphic.)
- They must have a homogeneous group (see 'General Regression Conditions' for graphics).
- The residuals must be independent. You can tell this from the Standardized Residual plot: if there is no pattern in the data (for instance, an upward trend), then they are independent. (See 'General Regression Conditions' for graphic.) If this condition is not met, you may need to run a time series analysis

"How to" in Excel

1. To make a scatter plot, highlight the two data sets of interest, then select *insert* > scatter. Choose upper left option. If you notice an exponential relationship, continue with this method.

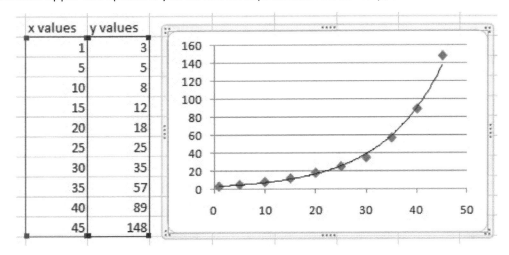

2. Use the formula "=ln(y)" to change your y values into *ln y* values. ("ln y" is the natural logarithm of y.) Create another scatter plot, and if you truly have an exponential relationship, the scatter plot of *x* and *ln y* will show a linear relationship.

x values	y values	ln y
1	3	=LN(C4)
5	5	1.609438
10	8	2.079442
15	12	2.484907
20	18	2.890372
25	25	3.218876
30	35	3.555348
35	57	4.043051
40	89	4.488636
45	148	4.997212

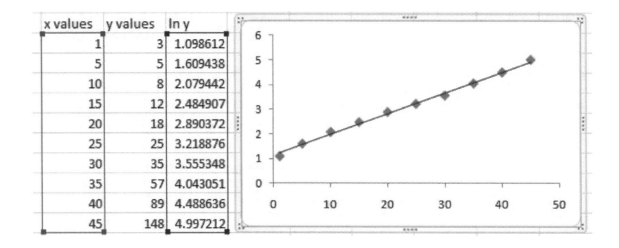

3. Using the *ln y* values as your new *y* values, do a linear regression analysis as explained in the linear regression section. This procedure is found in the How To section of Linear Regression.
4. Plug the coefficients found in the Linear Regression analysis into the exponential predictive model equation to get out predicted values: $y = e^{(Ax + B)}$ (to get the value of *e* from Excel, use the "=EXP()" function.)

Analysis

All the analysis for statistical significance and fit will be done according to the technique explained in 'Linear Regression.'

Warnings

All warnings are the same as those in the section for 'Liner Regression'.

Nonparametric Counterpart

If the normality condition is not met, you may want to use the nonparametric counterpart to this test. One popular nonparametric test that can replace any parametric regression test is MARSplines (Multivariate Adaptive Regression Splines). It doesn't impose the condition that any specific type of relationship exists between the variables (such as linear or exponential), can be used with multiple explanatory variables, and can even predict multiple outcome variables.

Logarithmic Regression

Predictive Model

The predictive model you will create in a logarithmic regression analysis looks like the following:

$$y = \ln(Ax + B)$$

Above, y is the outcome variable, and x is the explanatory variable. A is known as the coefficient of x, and B is a constant. This regression test will allow you to find the appropriate coefficient and constant values to define the relationship between y and x, allowing you to predict outcomes with specific x values.

Uses

Logarithmic regression is used to predict the response, y, from an explanatory variable, x, when x and y have a logarithmic relationship.

Example Questions Answered

- At what point in time will we see a significant decrease in responses from our mailer campaign?
- How long should we provide training on a specific task until we start seeing significantly less marginal benefit?

Conditions

- The x and y variables must be quantitative.
- The relationship between x and y must be logarithmic, as seen in the two scatter plots below.

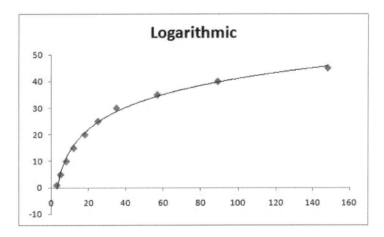

- *The logarithmic relationship will be transformed into a linear relationship* (see process below). *For that linear relationship, all the conditions of Linear Regression analysis must hold* (repeated below).
- Check for normality. (If normality is not met and your sample size is less than 50, you should use a nonparametric test like the one suggested at the end of this section.)
    - The y values must have a normal distribution.

- On a standardized residual plot, this is true if you see more values close to zero and less further away. (See 'General Regression Conditions' for graphic.)
    - If your sample size is over 50, it's less important that this condition is met.
  - The y values must have the same variance around each x.
    - Look at the best fit line on the scatter plot; this condition is not met if higher or lower values of x tend to be further from the best fit line than other values. (See 'General Regression Conditions' for graphic.)
- They must have a homogeneous group. (See 'General Regression Conditions' for graphics.)
- The residuals must be independent. You can tell this from the Standardized Residual plot: if there is no pattern in the data (for instance, an upward trend), then they are independent. (See 'General Regression Conditions' for graphic.) If this condition is not met, you may need to run a time series analysis.

"How to" in Excel

5. To make a scatter plot, highlight the two data sets of interest. Select *insert > scatter*. Choose the upper left option. If you notice a logarithmic relationship, continue with this method.

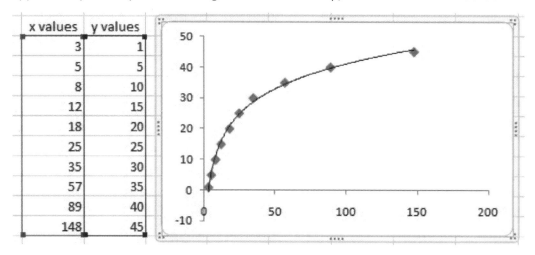

6. Use the formula "=ln(x)" to change your *x* values into *ln x* values. Create another scatter plot, and if you truly have an exponential relationship, the scatter plot of *ln x* and *y* will be linear.

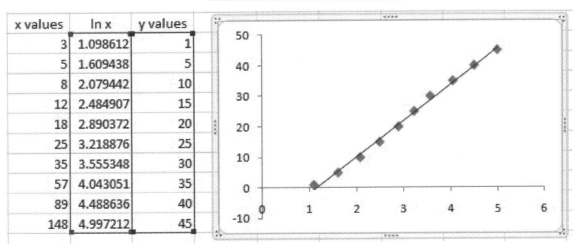

7. Using the *ln x* values as your new *x* values, do a linear regression analysis as explained in the linear regression section. This procedure is found in the How To section of Linear Regression.
8. Plug the coefficients found in the Linear Regression analysis into the exponential predictive model equation "y = ln(Ax + B)".

Analysis

All the analysis for statistical significance and fit will be done according to the technique explained in 'Linear Regression'.

Warnings

All warnings are the same as the section for 'Liner Regression'.

Nonparametric Counterpart

If the normality condition is not met, you may want to use the nonparametric counterpart to this test. One popular nonparametric test that can replace any parametric regression test is MARSplines (Multivariate Adaptive Regression Splines). It doesn't impose the condition that any specific type of relationship exists between the variables (such as linear or exponential), can be used with multiple explanatory variables, and can even predict multiple outcome variables.

Polynomial Regression

Predictive Model

The predictive model you will create in a polynomial regression analysis looks like the following:

$$y = Ax^3 + Bx^2 + Cx + D$$

Above, *y* is the outcome variable, and *x* is the explanatory variable. A, B, and C are known as the coefficients of x, and D is a constant. The regression test will allow you to find the appropriate coefficient and constant values to define the relationship between *y* and *x*, allowing you to predict outcomes with specific *x* values.

Note that the predictive equation does not necessarily need, nor is it limited to, the number of terms shown in the example above. You could have any combination of variables raised to the first, second, third, fourth, etc. powers in a polynomial regression. In this manual, we will focus on having just one x variable, raised to the second and third power, but the procedure can also be used with different variables in the same equation as well (so you could potentially have an equation with two different x variables [x_1 and x_2] raised to different powers that looks something like $y = Ax_1 + Bx_2^3 + Cx_2 + D$).

Uses

Exponential regression is used to predict the response, *y*, from an explanatory variable, *x*, when x and y have a nonlinear, nonexponential relationship.

Example Questions Answered

- What is the appropriate amount of customer contacts per month to maximize sales?
- What should we set the price at in order to sell the maximum amount of a given product?

Conditions

- Variables must be quantitative.
- The relationship between the explanatory and response variables must be able to be explained by a polynomial model (examples below).
    - Note that if the highest power a variable is raised to in your equation is 2, you have a second order polynomial. If the highest power is 3, you have a third order polynomial, etc.
    - Note below how second order polynomials have one inflection point, and third order polynomials have two inflection points.

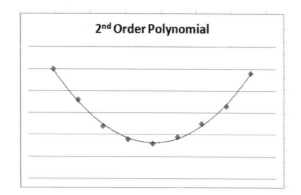
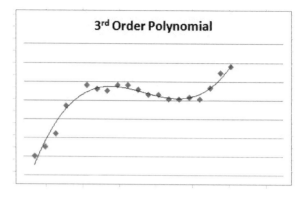

- Check for normality. (If normality is not met and your sample size is less than 50, you should use a nonparametric test like the one suggested at the end of this section.)
    - The y values must have a normal distribution.
        - On a standardized residual plot, this is true if you see more values close to zero and less further away. (See 'General Regression Conditions' for graphic.)
        - If your sample size is over 50, it's less important that this condition is met.
    - The y values must have the same variance around each x.
        - Look at the best fit line on the scatter plot; this condition is not met if higher or lower values of x tend to be further from the best fit line than other values. (See 'General Regression Conditions' for graphic.)
- They must have a homogeneous group. (See 'General Regression Conditions' for graphics.)
- The residuals must be independent. You can tell this from the Standardized Residual plot: if there is no pattern in the data (for instance, an upward trend), then they are independent. (See 'General Regression Conditions' for graphic.) If this condition is not met, you may need to run a time series analysis.

"How to" in Excel

1. To make a scatter plot, highlight the two data sets of interest. Select *insert > scatter.* Choose the upper left option.
2. To fit an equation once you have a scatter plot, right click on a data point, and then click *Add Trendline* and click on *Polynomial.* Start the *Order* box at two and work your way up until you find a good fit. Check the boxes for *Display equation on chart* and *Display R-squared value on chart.*

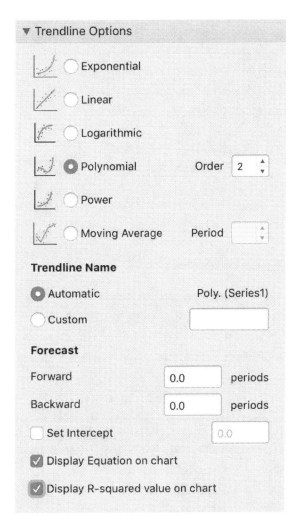

3. From the step above, you will already have a R^2 measure for goodness of fit and a predictive equation that can be seen on your plot.

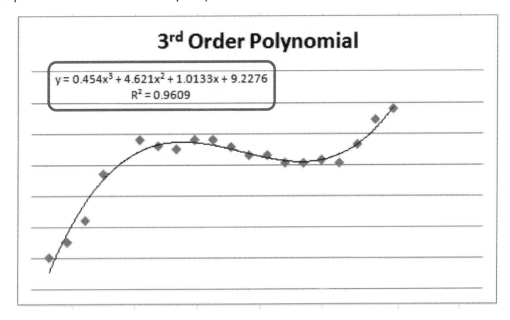

4. To get the full range of statistics (such as the p-values), follow the steps outlined below:
    - Create columns calculating each of the higher order terms found in the equation, as seen below. This chart will be used to run a regression with the Analysis ToolPak. As an example, for a third order equation the spreadsheet would look like this, with the x^2 and x^3 terms being calculated from the given x values:

x	x^2	x^3	y
-4	16	=P7^3	57
-3	9	-27	30
-2	4	-8	30
-1	1	-1	6
0	0	0	5
1	1	1	15

   - Now go to *Data > Data Analysis > Regression*. Highlight the y data for the *y input range* and all of the x data (including the columns you created) in the *x input range*.
   - Check boxes for *Standardized Residuals*. Click OK. All statistics as described and shown earlier will appear. Note that the coefficients mentioned for x variables 1–3 (which are x, x^2, and x^3, respectively) match those of the equation that was found earlier on the scatter plot: $y = 0.454x^3 + 4.621x^2 + 1.0133x + 9.2276$.

	Coefficients	Standard Error	t Stat	P-value	Lower 95%	Upper 95%
Intercept	9.227582171	10.82502632	0.85243	0.40738	-13.8454152	32.30057949
X Variable 1	1.013258428	2.107278618	0.480837	0.63757	-3.4782996	5.50481646
X Variable 2	4.621045489	0.595406035	7.761167	1.25E-06	3.351967572	5.890123407
X Variable 3	0.453997705	0.041592349	10.91541	1.56E-08	0.365345712	0.542649698

Analyze the Results

p-value

If any of the coefficients or the intercept has a p-value that is greater than .05, that specific coefficient or constant is not valid in predicting y. It should not be used in the predictive equation.

R^2 Adjusted

This is the percentage of variability in *y* that is explained by the *x* variables. Here you want to use the adjusted value because it corrects for the fact that you have more than one explanatory variable.

Confidence Interval

The range in which you are 95% sure the response variable *y* will be in at the given *x* values. See the confidence interval section under 'Linear Regression' to see how to find the confidence interval.

Warnings

- Keep the polynomial to the smallest order possible (meaning that if you can get a good fit by using an x^3, it's not necessary to try for a really good fit with an x^5). The higher the order, the

greater the possibility of overfitting. (Overfitting will cause your model to fit the specific sample data set so well that it won't be able to predict for the whole population.) To avoid this, start with the lowest polynomial order, and then work your way up until you have a suitable fit.
- Watch for Outliers.

Nonparametric Counterpart

If the normality condition is not met, you may want to use the nonparametric counterpart to this test. One popular nonparametric test that can replace any parametric regression test is MARSplines (Multivariate Adaptive Regression Splines). It doesn't impose the condition that any specific type of relationship exists between the variables (such as linear or exponential), can be used with multiple explanatory variables, and can even predict multiple outcome variables.

Time Series

Predictive Model

Any of the regression models described previously can be used to describe the trend in a time series analysis. The model you choose to use will depend on what the trend portion of the data dictates. For convenience, the possible predictive models are repeated below:

- Linear: $y = Ax + B$
- Multivariate Linear: $y = Ax_1 + Bx_2 + C$
- Exponential: $y = e^{(Ax + B)}$
- Logarithmic: $y = \ln(Ax + B)$
- Polynomial: $y = Ax^3 + Bx^2 + Cx + D$

Uses

Find and predict specific trends or seasonality of a response variable, y, according to time (the x variable).

Example Questions Answered

- How many sales are we likely to have in the next year?
- How much do the specific months of the year affect our close rates?

Conditions

- The response variable, y, must be quantitative, and the explanatory variable must be a unit of time
- If there is no seasonality, or you have removed the seasonality from your data, then all of the conditions of the regression model you are using apply, except for one—the condition of independence on the standardized residuals. In more advanced techniques, this condition would be dealt with, but for simple time series analysis in Excel it will be ignored.

"How to" in Excel

1. Time series analyses are typically more advanced than the scope of this text, but for a basic time series analysis there are two steps: one, identify the trend, and two, identify seasonality.
2. Look for a trend component.
    a. Perform a regression model according to the trend you see in the data (linear, exponential, logarithmic, or polynomial). For "How to" steps on performing the regression that you have chosen to fit the trend to, see that section of this guide.
        i. If the trend is hard to see, try taking a moving average to help you identify it.
        ii. Keep in mind that the R^2 may be low and the p-values may be high because the seasonality of the data is throwing off these statistics. You should not hold this type of regression to the same stringent conditions that others are subject to in order to identify a trend.

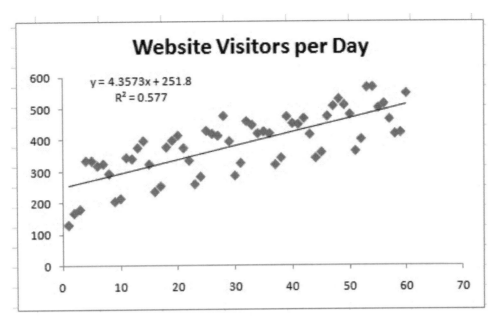

b. This equation can then be used to predict future values, with respect to the seasonality aspect of the data.

3. Look for a seasonal component. There are many approaches to finding seasonal components in a time series that are beyond the scope of this text. For our purposes, we will use the most basic method—looking at the data in the scatter plot and noticing repeating patterns. Once you notice at what intervals the pattern is repeated, you can do some segmentation to remove the seasonality, as seen in the example steps below.

4. How to use segmentation to remove seasonality:
    a. As an example, the data below is in days, and you can see it has a pattern in intervals of seven. (This makes sense, because seven days make up a week.)

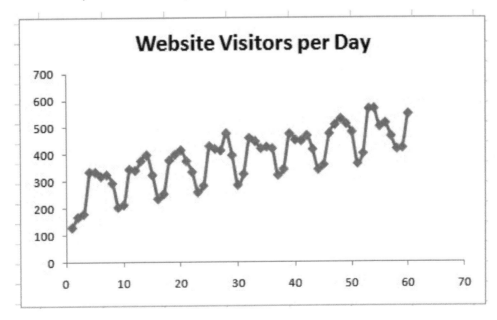

b. To describe these fluctuations in a quantitative manner, one option is to group the data according to the seasonal pattern you have found. For instance, below the data have been separated into weekdays and weekends. You will notice the R^2 values are much higher than for the regression of the data set as a whole, and you can now use all the robust conditions in regression analysis to make sure your conclusions are valid because the seasonal component has essentially been removed for each of the two new data sets. The equations found from regression analysis on these two different data sets can then be used to predict the website traffic in the future for weekdays or weekends, respectively.

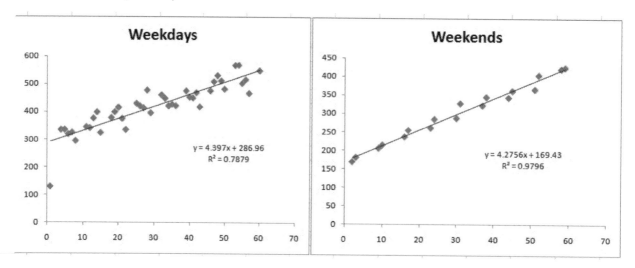

Moving Average

A moving average is often used to smooth out a time series analysis.

- To get a moving average, every data point's value is replaced by the average of it and a certain fixed number of data points behind it, which can be specified.
- You may want to use a moving average to smooth out the data and notice longer-term trends.
- Be aware that you could lose some seasonality in the data if you are using a moving average. The more points used in the moving average, the smoother the data become, but the more information is lost.

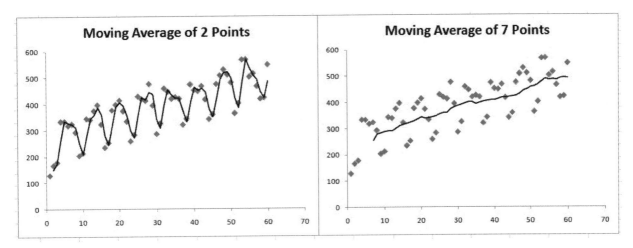

- To perform a moving average, first create a scatter plot of the data and then right click on a data point and click *Add Trendline*. Now click the button for *Moving Average* and set the *Period* to a suitable number. This will show you the line for the moving average on the plot.

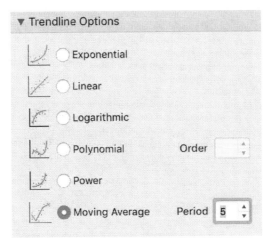

- To get the actual data points that make up the moving average line, go to *Data > Data Analysis > Moving Average*. Then, highlight the y values for the input range. Select an appropriate column for the output range, and type in how many points you want to be averaged per point in the *Interval* box. Click *OK*.

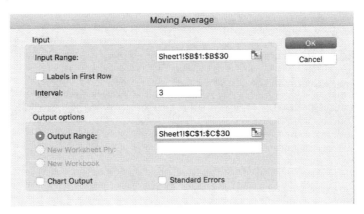

Logistic Regression

Predictive Model

The predictive model for logistic regression is an equation that outputs the probability that one of two outcomes will occur, as seen below:

$$P = (e^L) / (1 + e^L)$$

Above, P is the probability that one of two outcomes will occur. The value e is the natural logarithm base, approximately equal to 2.718. The value L is the logit, which takes the familiar form of a multivariate linear regression equation:

$$L = Ax_1 + Bx_2 + C$$

Again, you can use as many or as few x variables in this portion of the equation as you need. If you use multiple x values, however, make sure and check for multicolinearity with a correlation analysis. (See the *Warning* section of Multivariate Linear Regression for more information.)

In this manual, we will only deal with logistic regression with one independent variable, so our equation will look like the following:

$$L = Ax + B$$

This predictive model creates an S-Curve, shown below. (Probability will be on the y-axis, and the explanatory variable on the x-axis.):

This is used in place of a line (as in normal regression) because

- probability must be a value between 0 and 1, and
- probability doesn't necessarily increase linearly with the explanatory variable.

Uses

Logistic regression finds the probability of a positive or negative response according to one or more quantitative explanatory variables.

Example Questions Answered

- Will someone of a given age respond to our marketing campaign?
- Will someone purchase this product given a certain price?
- Will someone who has not logged into your product for a certain amount of days cancel?
- Will someone who has spent a given amount of time on your website purchase something?

Conditions

- Explanatory variables must be quantitative.
- Thee response variable must be binary (meaning only two responses are possible, such as a "yes" and "no" situation).

"How to" in Excel

We'll go through the process of doing all of the calculations for this type of regressions step by step.

1. Enter in the explanatory and response variable data (*x* and *y*) into a spreadsheet. Give the categorical data for *y* a numerical value of 1 and 0 (below, "yes"=1 and "no"=0). Then enter guesses for the coefficients of your equation. (It is not critical that these are extremely accurate—you just need to be in the right ballpark.)

Coefficients	
Constant	0.1
X	0.1

X	Y
20	0
23	0
24	0
25	0
25	1

2. Enter a formula to calculate the *logit*, or *L*, portion of the probability equation. (*Remember this is L = Ax + B.*)

	A	B	C
1	Coefficients		
2	Constant	0.1	
3	X	0.1	
4			
5			
6	X	Y	L
7	20		=$B$2+$B$3*A7
8	23	0	2.40
9	24	0	2.50
10	25	0	2.60
11	25	1	2.60

3. Enter a formula to calculate the natural logarithm base e raised to the logit. (*This will be Exp(L).*)

	A	B	C	D
1	Coefficients			
2	Constant	0.1		
3	X	0.1		
4				
5				
6	X	Y	L	e^L
7	20	0	2.10	=EXP(C7)
8	23	0	2.40	11.02
9	24	0	2.50	12.18
10	25	0	2.60	13.46
11	25	1	2.60	13.46

4. Enter a formula for the probability equation. (*This is $e^L/(1+e^L)$.*)

	A	B	C	D	E
1	Coefficients				
2	Constant	0.1			
3	X	0.1			
4					
5					
6	X	Y	L	e^L	Probability
7	20	0	2.10	8.17	=D7/(1+D7)
8	23	0	2.40	11.02	0.92
9	24	0	2.50	12.18	0.92
10	25	0	2.60	13.46	0.93
11	25	1	2.60	13.46	0.93

5. Enter a formula for the function that must be maximized. (*This is $y^{probability}*(1-probability)^{(1-y)}$.*)

	A	B	C	D	E	F	L
1	Coefficients						
2	Constant	0.1					
3	X	0.1					
4							
5							
6	X	Y	L	e^L	Probability	Function	
7	20	0	2.10	8.17		=(E7^B7)*(1-E7)^(1-B7)	
8	23	0	2.40	11.02	0.92	0.08	
9	24	0	2.50	12.18	0.92	0.08	
10	25	0	2.60	13.46	0.93	0.07	
11	25	1	2.60	13.46	0.93	0.93	

6. Enter a formula to calculate the natural logarithm of this function. (*This is ln(function).*)

	A	B	C	D	E	F	G
1		Coefficients					
2	Constant	0.1					
3	X	0.1					
4							Sum of ln(Function)
4							-230.94
5							
6	X	Y	L	e^L	Probability	Function	ln(Funtion)
7	20	0	2.10	8.17	0.89	0.11	=LN(F7)
8	23	0	2.40	11.02	0.92	0.08	-2.49
9	24	0	2.50	12.18	0.92	0.08	-2.58
10	25	0	2.60	13.46	0.93	0.07	-2.67
11	25	1	2.60	13.46	0.93	0.93	-0.07

7. Enter a formula to sum up all of these natural logarithms, which will be used later to calculate the equation coefficients. (*This is just a summation of the column you just created.*)

	A	B	C	D	E	F	G
1		Coefficients					
2	Constant	0.1					
3	X	0.1					
4							Sum of ln(Function)
4							=SUM(G7:G106)
5							
6	X	Y	L	e^L	Probability	Function	ln(Funtion)
7	20	0	2.10	8.17	0.89	0.11	-2.22
8	23	0	2.40	11.02	0.92	0.08	-2.49
9	24	0	2.50	12.18	0.92	0.08	-2.58
10	25	0	2.60	13.46	0.93	0.07	-2.67
11	25	1	2.60	13.46	0.93	0.93	-0.07

8. Enter an if-statement formula to set anything over or equal to .5 to return a value of "1" and anything under .5 to return a value of "0." (*The formula in Excel is if(probability>.5,1,0).*)

	A	B	C	D	E	F	G	H
1		Coefficients						
2	Constant	0.1						
3	X	0.1						
4							Sum of ln(Function)	
4							-230.94	
5								
6	X	Y	L	e^L	Probability	Function	ln(Funtion)	Predicted Y
7	20	0	2.10	8.17	0.89	0.11	-2.22	=IF(E7>0.5,1,0)
8	23	0	2.40	11.02	0.92	0.08	-2.49	1
9	24	0	2.50	12.18	0.92	0.08	-2.58	1
10	25	0	2.60	13.46	0.93	0.07	-2.67	1
11	25	1	2.60	13.46	0.93	0.93	-0.07	1

9. Enter a formula to see if your predicted value matches the true value. (*The formula in Excel is if(y=predicted y,1,0).*)

	A	B	C	D	E	F	G	H	I
1	Coefficients								
2	Constant	0.1							
3	X	0.1					Sum of ln(Function)		
4							-230.94		
5									
6	X	Y	L	e^L	Probability	Function	ln(Funtion)	Predicted Y	Match?
7	20	0	2.10	8.17	0.89	0.11	-2.22		=IF(B7=H7,1,0)
8	23	0	2.40	11.02	0.92	0.08	-2.49	1	0
9	24	0	2.50	12.18	0.92	0.08	-2.58	1	0
10	25	0	2.60	13.46	0.93	0.07	-2.67	1	0
11	25	1	2.60	13.46	0.93	0.93	-0.07	1	1

10. Enter a formula to give you the <u>% of concordant pairs.</u> (*This is the sum of the number of correct predictions divided by the total number of predictions.*)

	A	B	C	D	E	F	G	H	I	J	K	L
1	Coefficients											
2	Constant	0.1										
3	X	0.1					Sum of ln(Function)					
4							-230.94					
5												
6	X	Y	L	e^L	Probability	Function	ln(Funtion)	Predicted Y	Match?		Concordant Pairs	
7	20	0	2.10	8.17	0.89	0.11	-2.22	1			=SUM(I7:I106)/COUNT(I7:I106)	
8	23	0	2.40	11.02	0.92	0.08	-2.49	1	0			
9	24	0	2.50	12.18	0.92	0.08	-2.58	1	0			
10	25	0	2.60	13.46	0.93	0.07	-2.67	1	0			

11. Use Solver to find the equation coefficients. (Set up seen below.)
    a. Click *Data > Solver*.
    b. *Set Objective* or *Set Target* should be set to the cell where you calculated the *Sum of ln(Function)*.
    c. *By Changing Cells* or *By Changing Variable Cells* should be set to the current guesses you have for the coefficients.

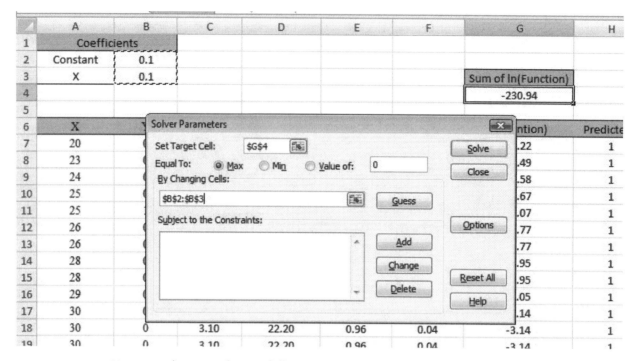

You may also see solver as follows, depending on your version of Excel:

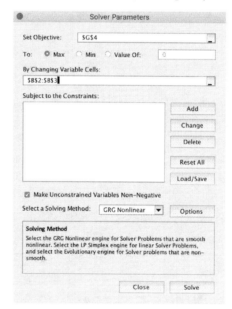

12. If you are not getting a good answer or Solver is not working, try two things:
    a. Change the initial guesses for the coefficients before running solver.
    b. Add some constraints to give the Solver better direction.

13. Now you have the coefficients in order to write the best fit probability equation, and you have the % of concordant pairs to know how well the equation fits.

	A	B	C	D	E	F	G	H	I	J	K
1		Coefficients									
2	Constant	-5.3094496									
3	X	0.11092102					Sum of ln(Function)				
4							-53.68				
5											
6	X	Y	L	e^L	Probability	Function	ln(Funtion)	Predicted Y	Match?		Concordant Pairs
7	20	0	-3.09	0.05	0.04	0.96	-0.04	0	1		74%
8	23	0	-2.76	0.06	0.06	0.94	-0.06	0	1		
9	24	0	-2.65	0.07	0.07	0.93	-0.07	0	1		
10	25	0	-2.54	0.08	0.07	0.93	-0.08	0	1		
11	25	1	-2.54	0.08	0.07	0.07	-2.61	0	0		

(Recall that the probability equation is $P = (e^L) / (1 + e^L)$ and the "L" in the equation is $L = Ax + B$, so the equation for the above data would be $y = (e^{0.11x - 5.31}) / (1 + e^{(0.11x - 5.31)})$.)

14. You can also plot the S-Curve by using the x variable as the x axis and the probability equation output as the y axis. This shows you where the change point is from a guess of 0 ("no" for below probability of .5) or 1 ("yes" for above a probability of .5) and how steep the curve is.

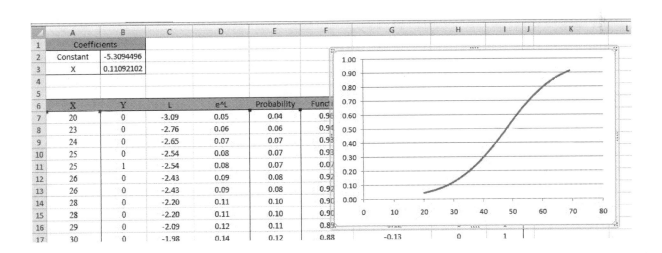

Analysis

p-value

Here, the null hypothesis for the p-value is backwards, *so the p-value must be greater than .05 for this model to be validated*. This is opposite of the other models we've discussed in this guide. Note that Excel does not give you the p-value, so you only have the % of concordant pairs that you can use to check the model against. Because of this, it is especially important to validate the model.

% of concordant pairs

This shows you how well the model fits the data—it tells you what percentage of predicted outcomes of 1 or 0 match the actual outcomes. Generally, 75% and above is accepted as a good fit.

ANOVA Overview

Uses

The ANOVA test is used to compare one quantitative variable against one or more categorical variables. It shows if the categorical variables have an effect on the mean of the quantitative variable.

Choosing the Appropriate Model

There are two different classes of the ANOVA test outlined below, each broken down further according to what kind of predictive model you are trying to build.

t-Test

This model is used if you have only one categorical variable that divides up the quantitative data into two sets. This is especially good for an experiment that looks at before/after effects. There are a few variations of the t-Test described further in the t-Test section. You can use a t-Test to analyze data like the data shown below:

 # Sales by Product

Product	
Product A	Product B
44	12
68	15
18	6
28	7
18	3

ANOVA

ANOVA is used when you have more than two means you want to compare. It is broken into two sections: the one-way ANOVA is used if you have only one variable you are testing for, while the two-way ANOVA is used to compare two different variables.

Here we must be clear on what we mean by the word *variable*. Taking the example of a one-way ANOVA, you could be testing the response rates of a marketing campaign broken down by promotion type. The "promotion type" is the variable, and each individual promotion type would give you a separate mean to test for (or separate column of data in the spreadsheet). If you also wanted to test to see if marketing channel had an impact as well as the promotion type, then you would use a two-way ANOVA. Promotion type and marketing channel are the two variables, and each value of these variables (promotion type A, B, and C, along with marketing channel X, Y, and Z) would give you a specific set of data points to test. Examples of data that can be analyzed using one- and two-way ANOVAs is shown below:

One-Way ANOVA

Sales by Product

Product		
Product A	Product B	Product C
25	44	12
140	68	15
12	18	6
26	28	7
5	18	3

(Above, "Product" is the categorical variable; Product "A," "B," and "C" are the values of this variable; and the columns of numbers are the quantitative data sets representing # of sales.)

Two-Way ANOVA

Sales by Product and Channel

Channel		Product		
		Product A	Product B	Product C
Channel A		25	44	12
		140	68	15
		12	18	6
		26	28	7
		5	18	3
Channel B		10	17	98
		46	10	335
		3	2	43
		11	13	112
		1	2	41

(Above, "Product" and "Channel" are the categorical variables; Product "A," "B," and "C" and Channel "A" and "B" are the values of these variables; and the columns of numbers are the quantitative data sets representing # of sales.)

Conditions

- The ANOVAs must have categorical explanatory variable(s) and one quantitative response variable.
- The variables must be independent of each other, meaning they don't affect each other. (This does not have to be true for a matched-pairs t-Test.)

o   As an example, take a person's height, age, and birth place. Height is dependent on age, so they are not independent. Birth place is not influenced by height or age, so it is independent of both of those variables.
- The data must have a normal distribution. (See How To below to check this.)
- Variances of the data sets must be equal. (This does not have to be true for a matched-pairs t-Test or a t-Test for unequal variances.)

How to Check Conditions in Excel

- To check normality in Excel, your best bet is to make a histogram of the data and see if it resembles a bell-shaped curve. Since there is not a standard statistical test in Excel for normality, you'll have to make a judgment call. We'll do this by creating a histogram.
- There are two ways to create a histogram in Excel. One way is by using the Data Analysis package, and another is by using the charting functionality.
    a. To use the Data Analysis method, do the following:
        i. First, create a range for the histogram bins in some cells next to your data. Generally, you want about 15–20 bins. Ensure that they are at equal intervals and that they cover the entire range of your data.

Data	Bins
98	0
335	20
43	40
112	60
41	80
25	100
35	120
6	140
1	160
12	180
121	200
81	220
98	240
32	260
11	280
36	300
46	320
66	340
37	
25	

   ii. Now go to *Data > Data Analysis > Histogram*. Highlight the data for the *input range*, and the bins you created for the *bin range*, and click *OK*.
   iii. The step above will output a "Bin" column and a "Frequency" column. The frequency column tells you how many times a value appears in each bin. To create the histogram, highlight the *Frequency* data, click *Insert*, *Column*, and choose a 2-d graph. (The histogram below does not have a normal distribution, as it does not resemble a bell curve.)

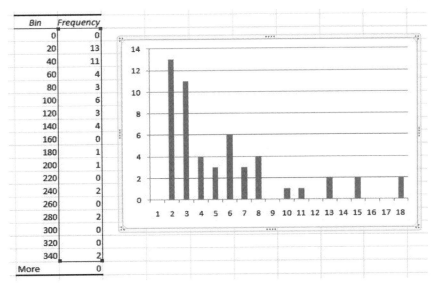

b. You can also create a histogram using Excel's charting functionality by doing the following:
   i. Click *Insert*, then the histogram chart, then select Histogram.

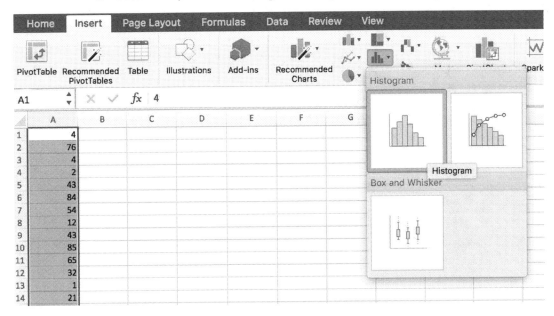

   ii. You can control the size of the bins by clicking *Format*, then the chart option, then changing *Bins* from *Auto* to *Bin width* and entering the size of the bins you would like.

- Now, to see if variances are equal, there are two things you can do in Excel:
    a. Use the VAR function to give you the variance of each data set and see how close they match. (If they differ by more than 10%, they are generally not considered to be equal.)
    b. For a more robust analysis, click *Data, Data Analysis*, and select the *F-Test Two-Sample for Variances*, and click *OK*. Select a data set range for each of the *Variable Range* boxes, and click *OK*.
        i. If the "F" value is further from 1 than the F Critical value, then the variances of the two sets are not equal. (In the graphic below, the variances are the same.)

	Variable 1	Variable 2
Mean	5.3	5.6
	7.566666667	
Observations	10	10
df	9	9
F	0.737012987	
P(F<=f) one-tail	0.32838538	
F Critical one-tail	0.409778892	

t-Test

Predictive Model

After performing a t-Test, you will be able to say whether or not two means from different data sets are statistically the same or different. This allows you to make qualitative predictions on how the two groups will perform, compared to each other, under a given set of circumstances.

 # Sales by Product

Product	
Product A	Product B
44	12
68	15
18	6
28	7
18	3

Uses

See how the means of two different groups compare. This is useful to see if the response variable changes after a treatment is given to a specific group, or to see how two different groups respond or perform in a certain situation.

Example Questions Answered

- Does gender affect the sales rate of our products?
- Does this medical treatment affect the blood pressure of our patients?
- Does this training course increase the efficiency of our staff?

Conditions

- You must have one categorical explanatory variable and one quantitative response variable.
- You must be comparing only two data sets.
- The data for each group must have a normal distribution. (See the How To section in "ANOVA Overview.")
- The variables must be independent of each other, meaning they don't affect each other. (This does not have to be true for a matched-pairs t-Test.)
    - As an example, take a person's height, age, and birth place. Height is dependent on age, so they are not independent. Birth place is not influenced by height or age, so it is independent of both of those variables.
- Variances of the data sets must be equal (unless it's a matched pairs t-Test or t-Test for unequal variances). You can check this by two methods:
    - Hypothesis test for equal variances. (Perform an F-Test, described in the "How to" section.)

- Find the variances of the data sets and compare them. (A difference of more than 10% is generally accepted as statistically meaning that the variances are different.) (You can use the VAR function in Excel to find the variance of each data set.)

"How to" in Excel

1. See the tutorial in 'ANOVA Overview' in order to check the above conditions and run an F-Test.
2. To run the t-Test test, click *Data, Data Analysis*, and according to the variance F-Test results and type of data you have, click on the appropriate t-Test.
   a. *Paired Two Sample for Means:* Choose this one if you are comparing a given population before and after a treatment.
   b. *Two-Sample Assuming Equal Variances:* Choose this one if the variances of the two samples are the same.
   c. *Two-Sample Assuming Unequal Variances:* Choose this one if the variances of the two samples are not equal. (For this case, you will usually have distinct subjects in each of the two samples.)

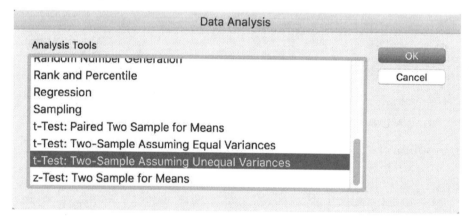

3. Highlight the two sets of data you are comparing for the two *Variable Range* boxes and click *OK*. The layout of the output is the same for all three t-Tests and is shown below. If the t-Stat is closer to zero than the t Critical two tail value (for most situations the two-tailed test is better to use than the one-tailed), then the means are the statistically the same. (In the graphic below, which is unrelated to the sample data shown above, the means are different.)

	Variable 1	Variable 2
Mean	128.75	5.25
Variance	472.9166667	7.583333
Observations	4	4
Hypothesized Mean Differ	0	
df	3	
t Stat	11.26808871	
P(T<=t) one-tail	0.000749396	
t Critical one-tail	2.353363435	
P(T<=t) two-tail	0.001498792	
t Critical two-tail	3.182446305	

If "t Stat" is closer to zero than "t Critical two-tail," then the means are statistically the same. In the image above, the means are different.

Warnings

Excel does not treat missing values in cells correctly when running these tests. Blank cells must be removed if you want to get correct results.

Analysis

p-value

A p-value of less than .05 in this case means that the two means are different. Note that Excel does not give a p-value for this test, so you must use the t-Statistic.

t-statistic

If the t-statistic is further from zero than the critical value, the means of the two populations are statistically different.

F-statistic

This is used for the F-test to find out if the variances of two samples are different. If the F-statistic is further from 1 than the critical value, then the variances are statistically different. This helps you decide which type of t-test to run for your data.

Nonparametric Counterpart

If the normality condition is not met, you will have to use the nonparametric counterpart to this test. A popular nonparametric test that can replace the t-Test is the Wilcoxon Signed-Rank Test. This uses the median as its measure of centrality, rather than the mean, and is therefore free from being skewed by having a non-normal distribution.

One-Way ANOVA

Predictive Model

After performing the one-way ANOVA test, you will be able to say whether or not two or more means from different groups are statistically the same or different. (For example, the means of the groups of data pictured below.) This allows you to make qualitative predictions about how the groups will perform, compared to each other, under a given set of circumstances. It also allows you to know if the categorical variable you are using has an effect on the outcome of the quantitative variable. (In the example below, the quantitative variable is "# of Sales" and categorical variable is "Product.")

Sales by Product

Product		
Product A	Product B	Product C
25	44	12
140	68	15
12	18	6
26	28	7
5	18	3

Uses

Compare the means of two or more groups that are broken down by a single categorical variable. For example, if I wanted to know how geographic location affected response rates, the categorical variable could be "state" and each data point within the state could be zip code response rate.

Example Questions Answered

- Which customer segments for a specific marketing campaign have the highest response rates?
- Which version of a mailer piece has the best response rate?
- Which traffic source to our website has the highest propensity for lead generation?

Conditions

- You must have one categorical explanatory variable and one quantitative response variable.
- The variables must be independent of each other, meaning they don't affect each other. (This does not have to be true for a matched-pairs t-Test.)
    - As an example, take a person's height, age, and birth place. Height is dependent on age, so they are not independent. Birth place is not influenced by height or age, so it is independent of both of those variables.
- The data for each group must have a normal distribution. (See the How To section in "ANOVA Overview.")
- Variances of the data sets must be equal. You can check this by two methods:

- Hypothesis test for equal variances. (Perform an F-Test, described in the "How to" section.)
- Find the variances of the data sets and compare them. (A difference of more than 10% is generally accepted as statistically meaning that the variances are different.) (You can use the VAR function in Excel to find the variance of each data set.)

"How to" in Excel

1. See the tutorial in 'ANOVA Overview' in order to check the above conditions.
2. Get the data into the right format. The example below shows what this transformation might look like:

Product	# Sales
Product A	25
Product A	140
Product A	12
Product A	26
Product A	5
Product B	44
Product B	68
Product B	18
Product B	28
Product B	18
Product C	12
Product C	15
Product C	6
Product C	7
Product C	3

Sales by Product

Product		
Product A	Product B	Product C
25	44	12
140	68	15
12	18	6
26	28	7
5	18	3

3. Click *Data > Data Analysis*. Choose *ANOVA: Single Factor*, and highlight all the columns of data that you want to run the test on. (In the above example, you would select columns for Product A, B, and C to compare their means.) Click 'OK'.
4. You will see the p-value in the output, shown below:

ANOVA

Source of Variation	SS	df	MS	F	P-value	F crit
Between Groups	3062.53333	2	1531.26667	1.28433236	0.31229784	3.88529383
Within Groups	14307.2	12	1192.26667			
Total	17369.7333	14				

5. Excel doesn't give you an R^2, but you can quickly calculate it with the formula shown below:

ANOVA							
Source of Variation	SS	df	MS	F	P-value	F crit	R-Square
Between Groups	3062.53333	2	1531.26667	1.28433236	0.31229784	3.88529383	=B12/B15
Within Groups	14307.2	12	1192.26667				
Total	17369.7333	14					

6. If the p-value is significant, it tells you that at least two of the means are statistically different, but it doesn't tell you which ones are different from each other. For this, you should conduct a multiple comparison test. For the purposes of this manual, we will look at box plots of the data to help us see which means appear to be different and those that might be the close to the same.

   a. Highlight the data, click *Insert*, then the histogram chart, then the *Box and Whisker* option.

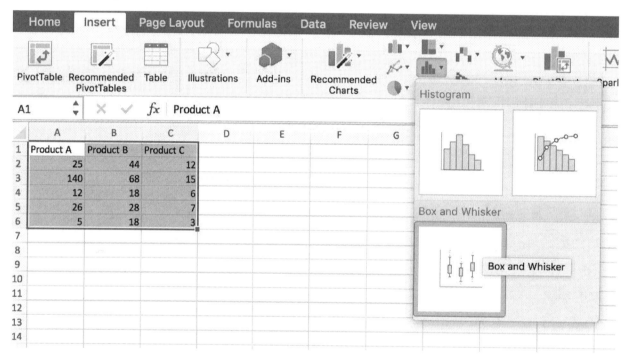

   b. Box plots are useful because they visually show you where the mean and median are in your data sets, and how the data is distributed. Below, we see that Product A (blue) has the greatest range in its distribution, but its median and mean are fairly similar to Product B (orange). Product C (grey) has the tightest distribution, and its mean and median appear to be significantly different from both Product A and B.

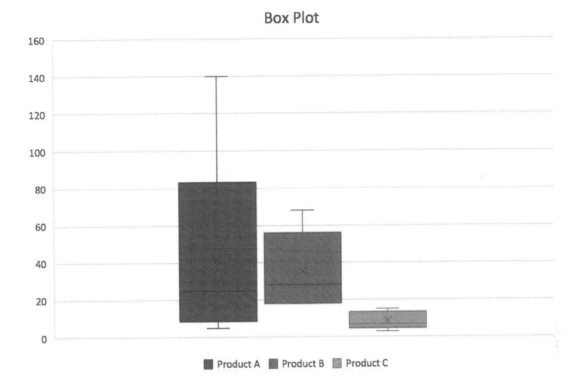

In the above chart, the center line in the boxes represents the median, and the x represents the mean, or average. The bottom and top of the boxes represent the 1st and 3rd quartiles, and the bottom and top whisker lines represent the minimum and maximum data point.

    c. Perform t-Tests between any two means you are questioning. So above, you could test between Product A and Product B to ensure statistically that they are the same, or between Product A and Product C to ensure statistically that they are different. See the Excel 'how to' section under the t-Test. (Warning: remember that each t-Test you perform has a 5% chance of being incorrect according to the p-value level. If you perform multiple t-Tests on the same data, then the chance that one of them will give you a false result will rise. So if you perform six t-Tests, you have a 26% chance that one of them will be wrong. (The formula to calculate this error probability being $1-(.95)^6$.)

Analyze the Results

p-value

A p-value under .05 in this case means that at least two of the means are different. It doesn't tell you which ones or how many. To find out which ones are different, specifically, you have to do some form of a multiple comparison test.

R^2

Tells you how much of the variation is due to the categorical variable. If you have a low R^2 it probably means that there are other factors that need to be considered in order to get a better fitting model. You could try a two-way ANOVA for this, or try a different variable in your model.

Nonparametric Counterpart

If the normality condition is not met, you might have to use the nonparametric counterpart to this test. A popular nonparametric test that can replace the one-way ANOVA is the Kruskal-Wallis test. As a follow up, the Wilcoxon Rank Sum test can be used in place of a multiple comparison test.

Two-Way ANOVA

Predictive Model

After performing the two-way ANOVA test, you will be able to say whether or not two or more means from different groups are statistically the same or different. This allows you to make qualitative predictions about how the groups will perform, compared to each other, under a given set of circumstances. It also allows you to know if the two variables you are using affect the outcome of the quantitative variable.

The advantage of the two-way ANOVA over the one-way is that interaction factors can be studied. Perhaps variable A and B don't have a large effect on the outcome by themselves, but when studied together they have a significant impact.

An example of data that can be analyzed with a two-way ANOVA is shown below:

Sales by Product and Channel

Channel		Product		
		Product A	Product B	Product C
	Channel A	25	44	12
		140	68	15
		12	18	6
		26	28	7
		5	18	3
	Channel B	10	17	98
		46	10	335
		3	2	43
		11	13	112
		1	2	41

Uses

Compare the means of data sets that are broken down by two categorical variables. For example, in the data pictured above, the two variables *Product* and *Channel* are breaking down the quantitative variable *# of Sales*.

Example Questions Answered

- What is the best combination of marketing channel and product to get the highest number of sales?

Conditions

- You must have two categorical explanatory variables and one quantitative response variable.
- The variables must be independent of each other, meaning they don't affect each other. (This does not have to be true for a matched-pairs t-Test.)

- o As an example, take a person's height, age, and birth place. Height is dependent on age, so they are not independent. Birth place is not influenced by height or age, so it is independent of both of those variables.
- The data for each set must have a normal distribution. (See the How To section in 'ANOVA Overview.')
- Variances of the data sets must be equal. You can check this by two methods:
  - o Conduct a hypothesis test for equal variances. (Perform an F-Test, described in the "How to" section.)
  - o Find the variances of the data sets and compare them. (A difference of more than 10% is generally accepted as statistically meaning that the variances are different.) (You can use the VAR function in Excel to find the variance of each data set.)

"How to" in Excel

1. See the tutorial in 'ANOVA Overview' in order to check the above conditions.
2. Set up the cells so Excel can run the test. One variable's values must be along the top row, and the second variable's values in the first column. Each data set within this grid must have the same number of data points. Below is an example:

Channel	Product	# Sales
Channel A	Product A	25
Channel A	Product A	140
Channel A	Product A	12
Channel A	Product A	26
Channel A	Product A	5
Channel A	Product B	44
Channel A	Product B	68
Channel A	Product B	18
Channel A	Product B	28
Channel A	Product B	18
Channel A	Product C	12
Channel A	Product C	15
Channel A	Product C	6
Channel A	Product C	7
Channel A	Product C	3
Channel B	Product A	10
Channel B	Product A	46

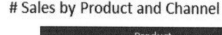

Sales by Product and Channel

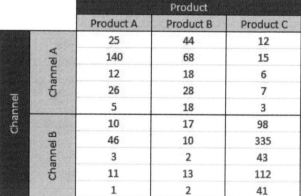

3. Click *Data > Data Analysis* and then choose *ANOVA: Two-Factor With Replication*, and input the number of rows each data set contains in the box labeled *Rows per sample*. (For the data above, you would enter five.) Make sure you highlight the column headers and row groupings, as seen below:

	A	B	C	D
1	Channel	Product A	Product B	Product C
2	Channel A	25	44	12
3		140	68	15
4		12	18	6
5		26	28	7
6		5	18	3
7	Channel B	10	17	98
8		46	10	335
9		3	2	43
10		11	13	112
11		1	2	41

Anova: Two-Factor With Replication

- Input Range: $A$1:$D$11
- Rows per sample: 5
- Alpha: 0.05
- Output options:
  - Output Range: $F$4
  - ● New Worksheet Ply:
  - ○ New Workbook

4. The relevant p-values will be visible in the output.

ANOVA						
Source of Variation	SS	df	MS	F	P-value	F crit
Sample	3349.63333	1	3349.63333	1.07763581	0.30957335	4.25967727
Columns	12074.4667	2	6037.23333	1.94228387	0.16526006	3.40282611
Interaction	34609.2667	2	17304.6333	5.56720411	0.01032151	3.40282611
Within	74599.6	24	3108.31667			
Total	124632.967	29				

Above, the p-value labeled Sample *(the first one) represents the variable in the rows.*

5. Now interpret the p-values. There are various relationships you could end up with, according to which p-values are significant and which are not. Below are graphs representing what each scenario could look like. *Each of the six points on each of the charts below represent what the averages of your data set groups could be.* The x axis represents one of the variables (in this example, product), and the color of the line the second variable (in this case, channel). The graphs are meant as a conceptual help to understand each of the possible scenarios. Here are the possible scenarios:

   a. If the interaction p-value is lower than .05, then the interaction of both variables affects the mean. If this is the case, none of the other p-values matter. (The individual contribution of each variable cannot be studied separately as a result of the interaction being significant.)

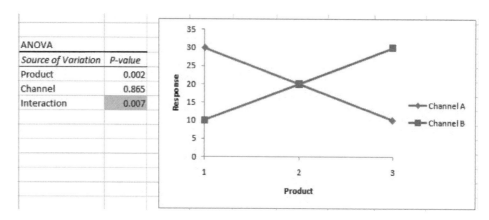

(Here, the mean changes according to both product and channel, and they each affect the outcome of the other.)

b. If the Interaction p-value is not significant, but the other two variables are, then each of the variables affects the mean, but the interaction between them does not.

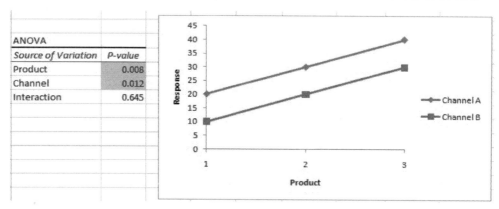

(Here, the mean changes according to both product and channel, and they do not affect the outcome of the other.)

c. If the interaction p-value is not significant, but one of the variables is, then only one variable affects the mean.

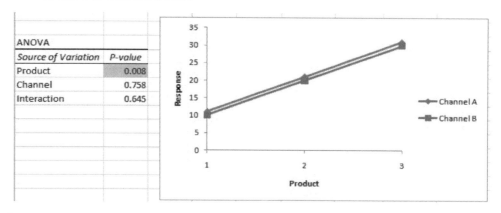

(Here, product is significant, so the mean changes across products, but not channels.)

or

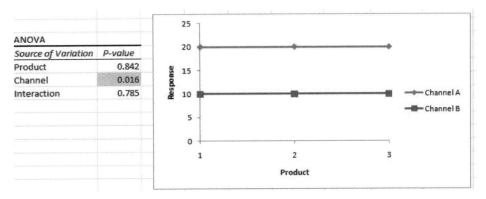

(Here, the product is not significant, so the mean does not change across products, but it does across channels.)

d. None of the variables are significant.

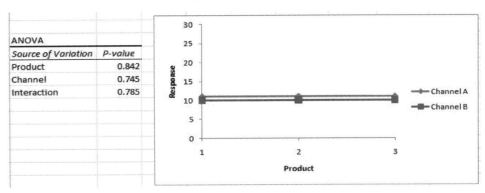

(Here, nothing is significant, so the mean does not change across products or channels.)

6. Excel doesn't give R^2 values, so you will have to calculate them, as shown with the equations below. (In this case you should use R^2 adjusted because you are studying more than one variable. Since Excel doesn't give this to you, just realize that the true R^2 will be slightly larger than what you calculate.)

ANOVA							
Source of Variation	SS	df	MS	F	P-value	F crit	R-Square
Sample	3349.63333	1	3349.63333	1.07763581	0.30957335	4.25967727	=B25/B$30
Columns	12074.4667	2	6037.23333	1.94228387	0.16526006	3.40282611	
Interaction	34609.2667	2	17304.6333	5.56720411	0.01032151	3.40282611	
Within	74599.6	24	3108.31667				
Total	124632.967	29					

Drag this formula down the next two cells to get the following R^2 values. Make sure you use the "$" for the *Total* cell so that its value does not change as you are dragging it down.

ANOVA							
Source of Variation	SS	df	MS	F	P-value	F crit	R-Square
Sample	3349.63333	1	3349.63333	1.07763581	0.30957335	4.25967727	0.02687598
Columns	12074.4667	2	6037.23333	1.94228387	0.16526006	3.40282611	0.0968802
Interaction	34609.2667	2	17304.6333	5.56720411	0.01032151	3.40282611	0.2776895
Within	74599.6	24	3108.31667				
Total	124632.967	29					

7. If any p-values are significant, you can look at box plots to see which averages might be different from each other.

   a. Put the data in a format that you can use to create a box plot, with each group in its own column.

Product A, Channel A	Product B, Channel A	Product C, Channel A	Product A, Channel B	Product B, Channel B	Product C, Channel B
25	44	12	10	17	98
140	68	15	46	10	335
12	18	6	3	2	43
26	28	7	11	13	112
5	18	3	1	2	41

   b. Highlight the data, then click *Insert*, then click the histogram icon, then the box plot option. *(If Excel doesn't interpret the data correctly, you can click on the chart, then click Chart Design on the ribbon, then Select Data to manually tell Excel which data you want in each group. See second image below.)*

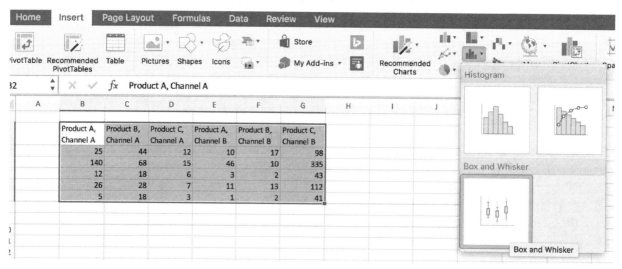

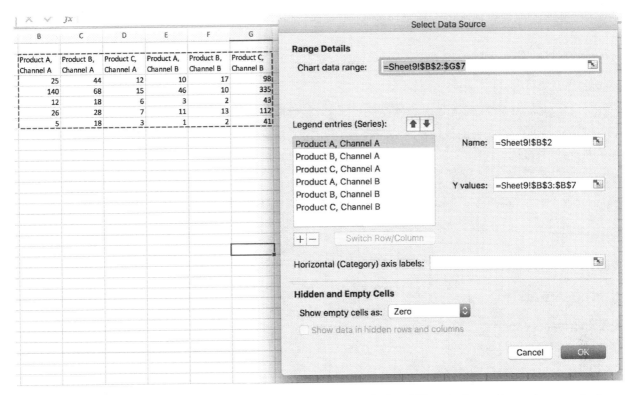

c. Analyze the box plot to see which means might be different than others. As a reminder, the middle bar in the box represents the median, the *x* represents the average or mean, the bottom and top of the box represent the 1st and 2nd quartile, and the bottom and top of the lines represent the min and max data values in that set. In the chart below, we might assume that the green bar has the highest average and the grey, yellow, and light blue have approximately the same average and are the lowest of the set.

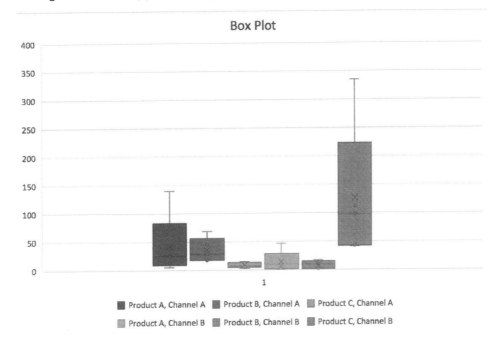

Analyze the Results

p-value

A p-value under .05 in this case means that at least two of the means are different. It doesn't tell you which ones or how many. To find out which ones are different, specifically, you have to do some form of a multiple comparison test.

Depending on which p-values are significant, it also tells you which variables have an effect on the means (or if the interaction between them does).

R^2

R^2 tells you how much of the variation in the means is due to the categorical variables.

Nonparametric Counterpart

If the normality condition is not met, you may have to use the nonparametric counterpart to this test. One option for a nonparametric test that can replace the two-way ANOVA is the Scheirer-Ray-Hare technique.

Chi-Square

Predictive Model

The Chi-Square test will produce a table of probabilities that can be used to predict categorical outcomes. For instance, in the sample table below that calculates percentages across the table, we can predict according to the data that if a person from Group A is asked for a donation, 84% of the time we expect them to say no.

	Donated?		
	Yes	No	Grand Total
Group A	16%	84%	73
Group B	68%	32%	13
Grand Total	41	45	86

Uses

The Chi-square is used to make predictions about categorical outcomes based on a table of percentages (as seen above).

Example Questions Answered

- Out of all of our customer segments, which ones are the most likely to buy specific products?
- What groups of people are most likely to be re-admitted to the hospital within 60 days?

Conditions

- All variables must be categorical.
- Cell counts must be at least five. Any count lower than that becomes unreliable in a statistical test because of a high degree of variability.

"How to" in Excel

1. First, put all the data into a two-way table using a pivot table. To do this, click *insert*, then *PivotTable*. Next highlight all of the data (must be categorical) you want to compare for the *Table/Range*. Click *OK*.
    a. Now place one variable in the *Row Labels* box and one in the *Column Labels* box. These are the two variables you will be comparing. Place the variable you are interested in counting in the *values* box and make sure that it is aggregating by *Count*. (If it's not, click on the field's arrow icon, click *Value Field Setting*. Click *COUNT*. Click *OK*.)

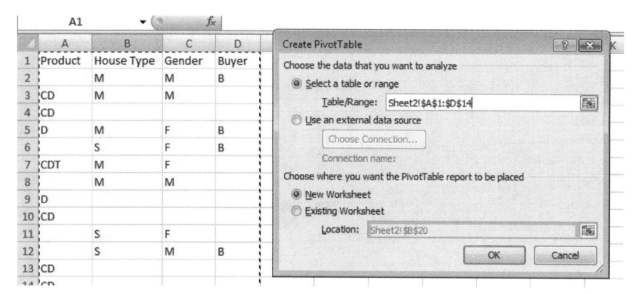

(Select all of the data and create a pivot table. Above, the B in the Buyer column represents someone who purchased, and a blank in that column means they did not purchase.)

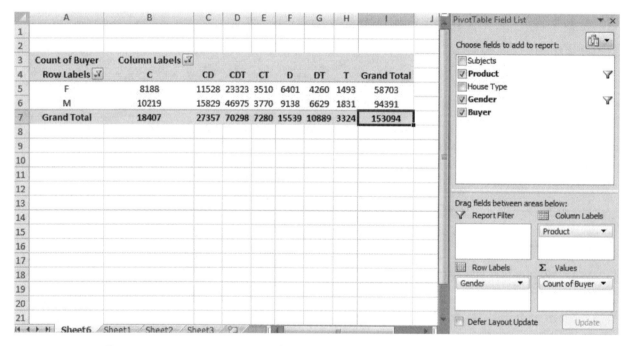

    a. If you want to compare more than two variables, drag them into *column labels* box, and turn off subtotals by going to *Design*, clicking *Subtotals*, and *Do not show subtotals*. (You could also put the extra variables in the *row labels* box, but this adds unwanted blank rows you would have to deal with later.)

2. Now we need to create a table that will be used as a comparison for the statistical test. Do the following to construct an expected outcomes chart:

a. Copy and paste all but the very top row of the pivot table. (This keeps the formatting, but it separates the table from the pivot data.) Delete all of the values in the table, with the exception of the totals (see below):

Count of Buyer Row Labels	Column Labels C	CD	CDT	CT	D	DT	T	Grand Total
F	8188	11528	23323	3510	6401	4260	1493	58703
M	10219	15829	46975	3770	9138	6629	1831	94391
Grand Total	18407	27357	70298	7280	15539	10889	3324	153094

Row Labels	C	CD	CDT	CT	D	DT	T	Grand Total
F								58703
M								94391
Grand Total	18407	27357	70298	7280	15539	10889	3324	153094

b. Create a formula that will calculate values that indicate perfect non-association between the variables being compared. The formula shown below will do this (you are multiplying row and column totals, and then dividing by the grand total), and you can drag it over and down to fill in the rest of the table. (Be sure and get the "$" signs in the right places, or the table will be incorrect when you drag the formula.)

Row Labels	C	CD	CDT	CT	D	DT	T	Grand Total
F	=$I12*B$14/$I$14							58703
M								94391
Grand Total	18407	27357	70298	7280	15539	10889	3324	153094

3. Use the CHITEST function to find the p-value.
   a. The table you just constructed will be your "expected range." The CHITEST formula, shown below, will output the p-value.

	A	B	C	D	E	F	G	H	I
1									
2									
3	Count of Buyer	Column Labels							
4	Row Labels	C	CD	CDT	CT	D	DT	T	Grand Total
5	F	8188	11528	23323	3510	6401	4260	1493	58703
6	M	10219	15829	46975	3770	9138	6629	1831	94391
7	Grand Total	18407	27357	70298	7280	15539	10889	3324	153094
8									
9									
10									
11	Row Labels	C	CD	CDT	CT	D	DT	T	Grand Total
12	F	7058.056625	10490	26955	2791	5958	4175	1275	58703
13	M	11348.94337	16867	43343	4489	9581	6714	2049	94391
14	Grand Total	18407	27357	70298	7280	15539	10889	3324	153094
15									
16		Chi Test p-value							
17		=CHITEST(B5:H6,B12:H13)							
18		CHITEST(actual_range, expected_range)							

4. If the p-value is less than .05, then the original table is statistically significant. You can therefore create some probability tables, from this original table, that can be used to predict future outcomes. There are three types of tables you can create to answer different questions—one calculated by row, one by columns, and one by both. We'll create all three below. To start, copy and paste all but the top row of the original pivot table. Do this a second time, deleting all the data values except for the totals, as shown below:

	A	B	C	D	E	F	G	H	I
1	Count of Buyer	Column Labels							
2	Row Labels	C	CD	CDT	CT	D	DT	T	Grand Total
3	F	8188	11528	23323	3510	6401	4260	1493	58703
4	M	10219	15829	46975	3770	9138	6629	1831	94391
5	Grand Total	18407	27357	70298	7280	15539	10889	3324	153094
6									
7									
8	Row Labels	C	CD	CDT	CT	D	DT	T	Grand Total
9	F	8188	11528	23323	3510	6401	4260	1493	58703
10	M	10219	15829	46975	3770	9138	6629	1831	94391
11	Grand Total	18407	27357	70298	7280	15539	10889	3324	153094
12									
13									
14	Row Labels	C	CD	CDT	CT	D	DT	T	Grand Total
15	F								58703
16	M								94391
17	Grand Total	18407	27357	70298	7280	15539	10889	3324	153094
18									

Now there are three types of probability tables you can create, depended on your purpose:

a. The formula below will create a **probability by *row*** table. (In this case, you will be able to say, "If you are a female, you have a _____% chance of buying product C.")

	A	B	C	D	E	F	G	H	I
8	Row Labels	C	CD	CDT	CT	D	DT	T	Grand Total
9	F	8188	11528	23323	3510	6401	4260	1493	58703
10	M	10219	15829	46975	3770	9138	6629	1831	94391
11	Grand Total	18407	27357	70298	7280	15539	10889	3324	153094
12									
13									
14	Row Labels	C	CD	CDT	CT	D	DT	T	Grand Total
15	F	=B9/$I15							58703
16	M								94391
17	Grand Total	18407	27357	70298	7280	15539	10889	3324	153094

b. The formula below will create a **probability by *column*** table. (In this case, you will be able to say, "If you buy product C, you have a _____% chance of being a female.")

	Row Labels	C	CD	CDT	CT	D	DT	T	Grand Total
8									
9	F	8188	11528	23323	3510	6401	4260	1493	58703
10	M	10219	15829	46975	3770	9138	6629	1831	94391
11	Grand Total	18407	27357	70298	7280	15539	10889	3324	153094
12									
13									
14	Row Labels	C	CD	CDT	CT	D	DT	T	Grand Total
15	F	=B9/B$17							58703
16	M								94391
17	Grand Total	18407	27357	70298	7280	15539	10889	3324	153094

    c. The formula below will create a **basic probability table.** (In this case, you will be able to say, "Out of the entire population, there is a ____% chance that you will find a female that buys product C.")

	Row Labels	C	CD	CDT	CT	D	DT	T	Grand Total
8									
9	F	8188	11528	23323	3510	6401	4260	1493	58703
10	M	10219	15829	46975	3770	9138	6629	1831	94391
11	Grand Total	18407	27357	70298	7280	15539	10889	3324	153094
12									
13									
14	Row Labels	C	CD	CDT	CT	D	DT	T	Grand Total
15	F	=B9/$I$17							58703
16	M								94391
17	Grand Total	18407	27357	70298	7280	15539	10889	3324	153094

5. Finally, you can summarize any of the above charts with bar graphs. This lets you see the differences in outcome probabilities visually. Just delete the contents of the *Row Labels* cell, highlight all the data as shown below, click *Insert*, and choose the visual you want. Bar charts are usually a good option.

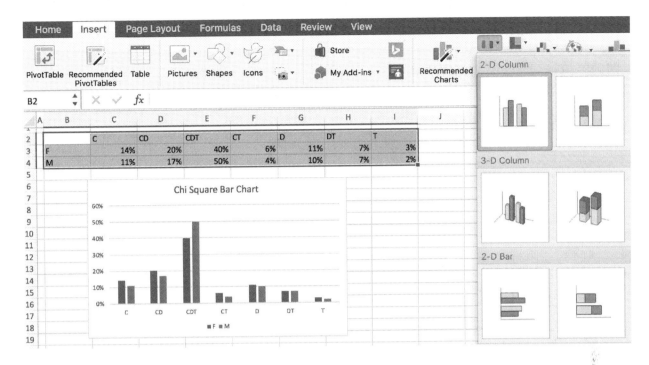

Analysis

p-value

If the p-value is below .05, then you can conclude that the variables have an effect on the outcome probability, and you can build probability tables from the original data table in order to predict categorical outcomes.

Probability Tables and Graphs

By looking at the probability tables and charts, you can visually see where the opportunities and problems may lie, and how large or small they are.

Warnings

Watch out for Simpson's Paradox

Simpson's paradox occurs when the conclusions of a Chi Square test switch upon addition of another variable. Let's take a quick fictional example. Suppose someone did a study to find out whether adults or children, upon given the opportunity, are more likely to give a wombat a hug. Looking at the table below, you would conclude that adults are more willing to hug these creatures.

	Hugged the wombat?		
	yes	no	totals
children	46	38	84
adults	86	38	124
totals	132	76	208

But what if we found out that the testing was being done with both an old and a young wombat? As it turns out, some people participating in the study were given the opportunity to hug a young one, and some the opportunity to hug an old one. Factoring that in, we see the following:

	young wombat		old wombat		
	yes	no	yes	no	totals
children	10	2	36	36	84
adults	73	19	13	19	124
totals	83	21	49	55	208

This table shows that while both children and adults have about the same likelihood of hugging a young wombat, the children will hug the old wombat more than the adults will. This means that children, as a whole, are actually more prone, in general, to hug wombats. (The fact that more adults happened to be tested with the easily huggable young wombat, while more children with the less huggable older one, accounts for the error in our first conclusion.)

Always look to the testing to see if there are potential lurking variables like the one above. Add them to your analysis in order to make sure you're not caught in Simpon's Paradox.

Conclusion

I hope this guide gives you a basic understanding of how to apply some basic modeling and statistical techniques to business problems you will encounter and how you can solve these problems with data. if you've had success using this manual, or if you have any questions, concerns, or feedback, please reach out to me on LinkedIn. (At the time of writing, I am the only "Curtis Seare" on LinkedIn.)

About the Author

Curtis Seare owns and runs an analytics training and consulting company, Vault Analytics (vaultanalytics.com). He also co-hosts a long-running podcast called Data Crunch (datacrunchpodcast.com) that makes topics in data science and machine learning approachable and interesting for professionals and business leaders. He lives in Austin, TX with his wife and daughter.